Leibniz and the Consequences

Jörg Zimmer

Leibniz and the Consequences

An Essay on the Great European Universal Scholar

Jörg Zimmer
University of Girona
Girona
Spain

This book is a translation of the original German edition "Leibniz und die Folgen" by Zimmer, Jörg, published by Springer-Verlag GmbH, DE in 2018. The translation was done with the help of artificial intelligence (machine translation by the service DeepL.com). A subsequent human revision was done primarily in terms of content, so that the book will read stylistically differently from a conventional translation. Springer Nature works continuously to further the development of tools for the production of books and on the related technologies to support the authors.

ISBN 978-3-476-05809-6   ISBN 978-3-476-05810-2 (eBook)
https://doi.org/10.1007/978-3-476-05810-2

© Springer-Verlag GmbH Germany, part of Springer Nature 2021

This work is subject to copyright. All rights are reserved by the Publisher, whether the whole or part of the material is concerned, specifically the rights of reprinting, reuse of illustrations, recitation, broadcasting, reproduction on microfilms or in any other physical way, and transmission or information storage and retrieval, electronic adaptation, computer software, or by similar or dissimilar methodology now known or hereafter developed.

The use of general descriptive names, registered names, trademarks, service marks, etc. in this publication does not imply, even in the absence of a specific statement, that such names are exempt from the relevant protective laws and regulations and therefore free for general use.

The publisher, the authors and the editors are safe to assume that the advice and information in this book are believed to be true and accurate at the date of publication. Neither the publisher nor the authors or the editors give a warranty, expressed or implied, with respect to the material contained herein or for any errors or omissions that may have been made. The publisher remains neutral with regard to jurisdictional claims in published maps and institutional affiliations.

This Palgrave Macmillan imprint is published by the registered company Springer-Verlag GmbH, DE part of Springer Nature.
The registered company address is: Heidelberger Platz 3, 14197 Berlin, Germany

Contents

Introduction 1

Leibniz in Context: The Life of a Universal Scholar 7

Leibniz and the Problem of Metaphysics 29

Leibniz Reception from the Enlightenment to Hegel 55

Perspectives on Leibniz 91

Unity in Diversity: Leibniz Today 109

Bibliography 133

About the Author

Jörg Zimmer The author studied philosophy and literature in Osnabrück and is Professor of Philosophy at the University of Girona, Spain, since 1997.

Introduction

Like no other thinker of his time, Leibniz had a finely developed sensitivity for writing occasions: his extensive correspondence shows particularly impressively the ability to adapt to his addressee in argumentation and language. Today, one would say: to pick him up where he stands. In the main philosophical writings, we see a systematic-principled diction that is missing in the extensive popular writings. Leibniz, however, had the claim that his statements directed at a general audience must be reformulatable at any time, even in metaphysical rigour. Speaking as generally understandable as possible in order to have a broad impact must not be done at the price of a loss of consistency. With this methodological awareness as a philosophical writer and the demand to leave the ivory tower of philosophy in order to make a difference with thoughts, Leibniz sets the bar quite high, if one wants to approach him also in the form of presentation.

The reader of this book should not expect a classical introduction, that is an overview of the entire work. He will certainly not find an academic monographic presentation, but rather a portrait, albeit not in the form of an executed painting, but rather as a portrait drawing that aims to sketch and characterize Leibniz and his thinking with a few strokes of the pen. The aim is to show Leibniz in his many facets *and* the systematic rigour of his basic idea, in the baroque diversity of his scientific and technical interests *and* the metaphysical unity of his concept of the world. Leibniz is to be shown in the context of his time-linked, however, with the question of what became of him in the history of his influence and what he can still mean today. Leibniz *and the consequences,* in this respect, mean two things: its history of reception and its topicality.

Reception processes have their own dynamics. In the later influence of a classical author, the historical content of his work is linked to the respective present, that is he moves through the course of history in constant transformation and in constant changes of perspective. This can be illustrated for the baroque period itself by a beautiful literary example. In his novel *Das Treffen in Telgte* (*The Meeting in Telgte*), Günter Grass describes the fictitious meeting of German Baroque poets in a small town near Münster and Osnabrück to discuss the future of the German nation in parallel with the peace negotiations taking place there at the end of the Thirty Years War. A member of Group 47, which is asking itself precisely this question about the new beginning in the post-war period of the war catastrophes of the twentieth century, *quotes* the historical past of a century that was also marked by the catastrophe of a great war. It is the century of Leibniz, and Grass paints an impressive picture of this time: a poet has also at one point taken up the "sword, called it his quill" and "wanted to know to whom he should first give it in writing" (Grass 1987, 14).

So there is correspondence between epochs, and when Leibniz's 300th birthday was celebrated in 1946, the political Leibniz, oriented towards peace and the reconciliation of interests, was much more in the foreground of the ceremonial speeches than ever before and afterwards. In changed contexts of reception, the basic ideas of a classical author thus take on new connotations in the changes of the course of time: subtle, sometimes quite gross shifts in meaning often take place. Theoretically, Walter Benjamin has reflected on this central significance of *reception history*. Significantly, in a section entitled "Monadology" in the "Epistemo-Critical Preface" to his book on Baroque tragedy, he speaks of the prior history and after-effects of the works. The idea of each work is monad and "contains the image of the world" (Benjamin 1974, p. 227 f.). For our context, this means nothing less than understanding Leibniz as an expression of his world. This is exactly what we will try to do in the first and second chapters.

According to Benjamin, however, it also means that between the work as an expressive form of its time and us there is the entire history of reception and interpretation. Therefore, by reconstructing these processes of reception we must develop an awareness of how these interpretations have shaped our own image. In a book about the reception history of the Baroque poet Martin Opitz, it is said in a methodologically very enlightening way: "Works that have had a lasting effect have in turn helped to shape the sociocultural tradition that still shapes contemporary reception. From this follows the imperative instruction to follow the process of the works' transmission in order to be able to examine the determinants of their current appropriation and, if necessary, to break their power" (Garber 1976, p. 12). The second and third chapters are to be understood in this sense: We must know the history of reception as a "consequence", at least in its main features, in order to be able to gain our own, as unobstructed as possible, relationship to Leibniz from the present. However, in understanding the history of reception, the awareness is sharpened that even the topicality of Leibniz is only a historically determined perspective on him.

In the *Arcades Project,* Benjamin has captured this necessary and inescapable perspective of our view of tradition in the apt metaphor of Libra: "Every historical insight can be visualized in the image of a pair of scales that stand up, one bowl of which is loaded with the weight of the past, the other with the insight of the present. While on the first one the facts cannot be gathered inconspicuously and not in sufficient numbers, on the second one only a few heavy, massive weights may lie" (Benjamin 1982, p. 585). We try to follow this thought in the structure of the presentation. The reconstruction of work and effect has more space, but not more weight: "Posthistory" becomes—also a motif in Benjamin's thinking reminiscent of Leibniz—the "force field" of the appropriation of a classic like Leibniz, "in that the topicality works into it" (Benjamin 1982, p. 587).

The topicality of Leibniz's thinking is the subject of the last chapter. The fact that his metaphysics starts out strictly from the individual and his perspective on the context of the whole makes it a possible starting point for the present day. For Leibniz thinks the individual substance *essentially* in relation to the others, the world, in other words, as a unit of all interactions of individual substances. Here lies the centre of the systematic basic idea, which excludes both closed systematics and arbitrariness. Leibniz's topicality thus consists, in a word, in thinking diversity and plurality without letting reality fall apart into the individual. He does not have a spelled out system, but he always thinks the fragmentary from the unity of a basic idea. Thousands of note sheets show, in contrast to narrow metaphysical main writings, the workshop character of Leibniz's philosophy, which is articulated in baroque abundance but never loses itself in the details. It is about giving the individual, its power and the relationships in which it stands, metaphysical basic status for our concept of world.

In the history of the reception of the philosopher Leibniz, the metaphysician and the logician have been at the forefront. Leibniz's political thinking was only contingently in the foreground on his 300th birthday, so to speak, because two epochal catastrophes, the end of the Thirty Years' War at Leibniz's birth in 1646 and the end of the Second World War, coincided here. However, the topicality of the political thinker Leibniz is not contingent, but arises from the connection with his metaphysics. And if in the twentieth century the historical correspondence lay in catastrophes, the epochal affinity in the twenty-first century can be seen in the fact that he allows an order of "compossibility", a political unity of the many to think. It is precisely our time that can discover the political thinker Leibniz: for it has the problem of having to think and shape unity in the multitude *politically*. At the end of the book, we will ask to what extent Leibniz' metaphysical basic idea can offer a normative framework and thus criteria for this.

For Leibniz, this plurality does not mean arbitrariness, but is understood as an ontological characteristic of the world. Compossibility is an ontological concept that expresses what is at the same time possible, that is politically speaking it aims at an order in which the individual realizations of freedom are not mutually exclusive but can exist together. This leads him, among other things, to think beyond the classical principles of natural law to a *principle of solidarity*: not only *suum cuique tribuere* and *neminem laedere, to* give to each his own and harm no one, but also to live with decency (*honeste vivere*) in a very specific sense: Leibniz concretizes this "unsubstantiated moral-philosophical general clause" (Holz 2013, p. 106) very concretely as *alios adiuvare*, as instruction to help others.

For Leibniz, politics is not, as in the classical political theory of modern times, the answer to the collision of claims to freedom and individual interests, but rather it starts from the very beginning from the idea of the *bonum commune*, that is from the common good or *common interests*. And in the one world in which we live today, the major problems, from the preservation of the common foundations of life to the solution of the global social question, cannot be tackled other than through criteria of balance. This idea of compensation through common interests is at the heart of Leibniz's political thinking. Another moment of great topicality is his always multilateral understanding of international politics: it is about adjustments in political constellations in the unity of a pluralistic interrelationship of forces.

Leibniz in Context: The Life of a Universal Scholar

When Gottfried Wilhelm Leibniz saw the light of day in Leipzig on June 21, 1646, negotiations to end the Thirty Years' War were taking place in Münster and Osnabrück. In 1648, the Peace of Westphalia marked the end of what was probably the greatest catastrophe in German history at that time. Golo Mann described these two "Westphalian cities of Münster and Osnabrück [...], this one as the residence of the Catholics, that one of the Protestants", as "islands of security and splendid prosperity in a sea of misery" (Mann 1991, p. 220). Leibniz was born into the post-war period of this war, the most devastating war in European history: "The consequences were bad for millions of suffering, martyred human individuals. They were also bad for the collective being, called nation, in its living together and competition with other nations" (Mann 1991, p. 228).

This war left behind a Germany that was politically fragmented, economically backward and divided along religious lines and will remain a backward country in European comparison for centuries to come. In his work and activities, Leibniz reacted to all these basic conditions of the epoch. The "community of a multiplicity of individuals is based on the principle of peacefulness" (Holz 2013, p. 20)—Leibniz followed this maxim throughout his life as a lawyer and diplomat and as a denominationally and politically irenic man. Unity in diversity will be the basic idea of his philosophy, and as an inventor and science politician he will work tirelessly to overcome Germany's backwardness.

But the circumstances of this time also gave rise to what Helmuth Plessner so aptly called the "late nation" as a historical long-term effect. For through its fragmentation into small states, Germany was one of those countries "which have not participated in the development of the modern consciousness of the state since the seventieth century", but which "through centuries of particularism and half-solutions" will only gain its national consciousness with the political romanticism of the early nineteenth century (Plessner 1974, p. 52 f.)—with again dire consequences, because the concept of "nation" is then not bound to a political concept of the state, but to ideas of national identity. These ideas will continue to have an effect until the catastrophes of the twentieth century and will be of no small importance for the reception history of Leibniz's ideas.

In terms of the history of science and philosophy, Leibniz was born into an era in which a new scientific view of the world was formed by Galileo, Kepler and his contemporary Newton—a development to which Leibniz reacted just as much as to modern philosophy, which also emerged in the seventeenth century and is characterised in all its classical forms by the subject as point of departure:

> In its two major lines of development, that of empiricism and that of rationalism, modern philosophy is characterized

by a turning towards the subject. [...] Locke's tabula rasa is the tabula rasa of the subject of knowledge, Descartes' meditations are the self-reflection of the individual thinking self. In Leibniz's philosophy, finally, this development culminates in the replacement of the two Cartesian substances or the one Spinozist substance by a substantiation of the individual. (Poser 2016, p. 15)

These developments of his epoch converge in Leibniz's thinking: he reacted to the challenge of the new scientific view of the world with the insight into the necessity of a unity of scientificity and metaphysical foundation of the concept of world, and to the turn of modern philosophy towards justification from the subject with a philosophical basic conception, which understands this subject not only as an individual, but at the same time as a *repraesentatio mundi*, that is an expression of the world as a whole—and thus insists that philosophy must not only be the justification of knowledge from the thinking self, but *also* the justification of a concept of world.

In the age of science, however, metaphysics, which is supposed to provide this justification, can no longer consist of the eternal certainties of the pre-scientific world view of the Middle Ages: "Philosophical systems can no longer lay claim to absolute truth. *Philosophy becomes a hypothesis*—and Leibniz did not present his system in any other way" (Holz 1992, p. 23). Leibniz thus combines the claim to scientificity with the speculative meaning of philosophy, in that metaphysical models must not contradict scientific knowledge. Both in terms of his work in the historical context of his time and his position in the scientific-philosophical situation of the epoch, Leibniz is what he himself said of the monad: a *miroir vivant,* a living mirror of his time, in which the contradictions and tendencies of modernity are presented in perspective. This makes him one of the most important personalities of the late seventeenth and early eighteenth centuries—the paradigmatic figure of the modern age, which continues to have an effect to this day and still has something to say to the present.

Childhood, Youth and Study Time

Leibniz was born the son of the lawyer and professor of moral philosophy Friedrich Leibniz. His mother Catharina, 24 years younger than her husband, was also the daughter of a well-known lawyer. Since Leibniz only began to make copies of his letters after his youth and to accumulate a vast amount of notes, which make up a large part of his extensive estate, the sources on his childhood and youth are thin. He lost his father as a child and was considered precocious. Already in his school days, he is said to have written a Latin poem of 300 hexameters. Because of his talents, he was allowed to use the extensive library left by his father as a child.

In 1661, at the age of less than 15, Leibniz began to study philosophy at the University of Leipzig, among others with Jacob Thomasius, whose son Christian would later become a famous representative of the German Early Enlightenment. Leibniz passed his baccalaureate examination in 1663 with a paper entitled *De principio individui*. In this work, Leibniz showed early on that he had the talent to become a significant philosopher, for the basic idea of his later metaphysics, to start from the individual, is already present in this very early work by a 17-year-old. After his baccalaureate, Leibniz went to Jena for a semester to study with the mathematician Erhard Weigel, with whom he not only learned mathematics but also came into contact with ancient Greek philosophy. Both influences will be of central importance for the development of his thinking, as Feuerbach already pointed out very emphatically:

> Erhard Weigel combined mathematics with Pythagorean philosophy and sought to link Aristotle with the newer philosophers. He mentioned Leibniz honourably in several places in his writings. He had a particularly stimulating effect on him and caused him to develop his own thoughts, especially in mathematics, as well as to invent his binary arithmetic. Brucker, in his 'Vita Leibnitii', believes that it is also to be attributed to this man that Leibniz had the idea of mediating the old philosophy with the newer one at an early stage. But this idea [...] must at the same time be regarded as a property of Leibniz. (Feuerbach 1984, p. 15)

Here an important story that will still occupy us is alluded to: the Rosental story, which Leibniz tells in a late letter to Nicolas Remond in his old age (W V, 321). We do not want to quote it at this point, but rather introduce it for the time as an example of the early independence of his thinking. Old Leibniz remembers how, as a 15-year-old, he went for a walk in the woods of Rosental near Leipzig to think about whether he should stick to the substantial forms (i.e., Aristotle) in philosophy. This will be decisive for the development of his metaphysics. And it is an astonishing testimony to independent thinking: for it means nothing less than to insist on the importance of tradition—at the age of just 15!—against the anti-scholastic impulse of an entire epoch that considers Aristotleism obsolete.

After the time in Jena, Leibniz returned to the University of Leipzig and studied law from then on. There he was not accepted for a doctorate because he was considered too young for it. Therefore, in 1667 he submitted his dissertation on the problem of insoluble legal cases to the Franconian University of Altdorf, where it was considered so outstanding that he was offered a professorship. He did not accept it. His life was to take other paths.

In 1667, Leibniz met the baron Johann Christian von Boineburg, who encouraged him to write a paper on new methods of teaching law. Von Boineburg, who had been in the service of the Elector of Mainz, arranged for Leibniz to contact Johann Philipp von Schönborn on the basis of this paper. The Elector of Mainz was also chairman of the electoral college and provided the chancellor in the Holy Roman Empire of the German Nation. As early as 1670, Leibniz, who had entered Schönborn's service, was commissioned to create a cross-denominational body of laws at the Electoral Court of Appeal in Mainz, which had jurisdiction over the entire empire. In Mainz, one of the three ecclesiastical electorates, there was an interest in the reunification of the Christian denominations. This irenic denominational policy is a further life theme of Leibniz, which was already laid out in his youth.

Productive Years in Paris

In 1672, the Elector sent his lawyer Leibniz, who had in the meantime risen to the position of councillor, on a secret diplomatic mission to Paris. There he was to present his *Consilium Aegyptiacum*, his famous Egyptian plan to persuade King Louis XIV to launch a campaign against Egypt. We will come back to this. But what is a diplomat doing in Paris on a secret special mission? He waits for opportunities to penetrate further and further with this intention, and that means he has plenty of time. Leibniz used this time in Paris and his first trip to London to make contact with international science: "Meeting men like Huygens, Colbert, Malbranche and Arnauld in Paris, Oldenburg, Boyle and Newton, allowed Leibniz to catch up with the scholarly republic" (Poser 2016, p. 19).

During the Paris years Leibniz will work out the basic principles of his infinitesimal calculus in 1675. This will lead to Newton's accusation of plagiarism many years later. The *Royal Society* decided this priority dispute against Leibniz in London in 1712. However, Leibniz apparently arrived at his result in a different way than Newton's fluxion calculus. Today, there is scientific agreement that Newton and Leibniz independently of each other arrived at their results, which revolutionized mathematics, science and technology.

Leibniz also made his first public appearance as a technician in Paris. In the Paris years, he developed his mechanical calculating machine for the four basic arithmetic operations. For this project in Paris, he was able to work together with important precision mechanics of his time, and when he demonstrated the calculating machine in the *Royal Society in* 1673 during his trip to London, people there were so impressed that he was accepted into the learned society. Technical problems remained as with all his inventions: What is important, however, is not whether or not the tenner transmission of the calculating machine worked or not, but the basic idea: "As a young man, Leibniz had the decisive idea of using a graduated roller to solve the problem of building a *calculating machine* for all four basic arithmetic operations. [...] The graduated roller was used in the construction of mechanical calculating machines until 1957. Leibniz also invented *dual numbers*, the basis of all computer technology, and designed two completely different calculating machines and a number converter from dual to decimal numbers" (Poser 2016, p. 425). Leibniz had problems in implementing his inventions due to the technical state of his time, but the thoughts behind these inventions were far beyond their time; they were visionary and innovative.

And the Egyptian plan? Leibniz had developed it in an extensive memoir. It convinced von Boineburg so much that he provided Leibniz with personal letters of recommendation to the First Minister of Louis XIV. Leibniz wanted to convince the French king of the strategic importance of Egypt for a hegemonic position in the Mediterranean and for trade relations with the Orient and the Far East. He was thinking in a pan-European way, that is what consequences such a shift in power would have for the balance and equilibrium between the European powers. Of course, from today's point of view one must criticize that for political goals in Europe one cannot simply propose to occupy an African country. But critical thoughts on Eurocentrism did not lie in the political horizon of the seventeenth century, so there is no point in criticising Leibniz at this level, even though one will of course judge differently today.

Rather, one must remember the systematic-strategic basic idea underlying the Egyptian plan: When Leibniz ran it in Paris, France, as the continental hegemonic power in Europe that emerged from the Thirty Years' War, was about to wage war against the Netherlands. Leibniz wanted to bind French forces in Egypt to take pressure off the Netherlands. At the same time, a commitment in the Orient meant putting pressure on the Ottoman Empire, which was seeking to expand into Europe from the south-east. And that in turn meant taking pressure off the German Empire, whom he represented diplomatically, so to speak. Leibniz thus shows that he is certainly thinking geopolitically in a very modern sense and is not oriented towards a single interest. So behind the Egyptian plan is an understanding of international politics that we would call multilateral today. Leibniz always proceeded from constellations in which a unity is created in a pluralistic context and changed through political action.

Ultimately, it is his basic philosophical concept of interacting forces that is also behind his understanding of political action:

> The pluralism of states and interests was as indispensable to him as the diversity of substances. But just as he undertook to summarize this diversity in the material world as order and integration and superior structures, [...] so he was also concerned with the plurality of states and interests. He wanted to bring them into such a relationship with each other that they would become compossible, that is, they would not contradict each other without necessarily agreeing. [...] The harmonization of the world into composite structures does not mean the elimination of diversity, of differentiated multiplicity; it only strives for its integration in a higher level of structure. The 'Egyptian Plan' was thus based on the idea of such a structuring of the European world. (Holz 2013, p. 244 f.)

Consequently, in the *Consilium Aegyptiacum,* the young Leibniz already articulates in essence the basic idea of his lifelong political thought and action—and as such an early witness, the plan is interesting and worthy of consideration, not as a testimony to princely servitude and early Eurocentrism in European modernity. The plan failed, France led its campaign against the Netherlands, and it is not known whether the memorandum, beyond Minister Pomponne, even reached the hands of Louis XIV. Only its epilogue falls at the beginning of the nineteeth century, at a time when it is indeed necessary to speak clearly of colonialism: Napoleon was in Egypt. He probably had no knowledge of Leibniz's old plan, which somewhere in the archives of the French ministerial bureaucracy was exposed to the gnawing criticism of mice. But with Napoleon in Giza, however, Leibniz's idea that the Mediterranean Sea was controlled from Egypt also gained acceptance, although unknown to him. The *mare nostrum* is a meeting point of three continents and a unique space for the exchange of goods and cultures. Leibniz's ideas still remain real in the construction of the Suez Canal, and the Mediterranean is still today (just think of the migration problem) a geopolitical and strategic problem of the first order. The Egyptian plan is therefore more than a curiosity, even if it failed.

Detours to Hanover

While Leibniz was still in Paris, von Boineburg and the Elector of Mainz died. Leibniz was thus unemployed. In 1676, he entered the service of the Guelph Duke Johann Friedrich von Brunswick-Lüneburg and travelled via London and the Netherlands to the royal residence of Hanover. Leibniz was now 30-year-old and was to remain in Hanover until the end of his life. He would repeatedly escape from Hanover and embark on extended journeys, some of which were expressly forbidden by his employer, in order to escape the confines of the province to Italy, Vienna or Berlin. One can say that Leibniz did not only arrive in Hanover by detours, but that he also stayed in Hanover by detours.

The famous story of the meeting with Spinoza must be told at this point:

> [Spinoza] wore the somewhat scraped working clothes of a craftsman, his complexion had little of the darkness of the Portuguese Jews, but was pale, he looked ill. [...] Spinoza pulled up a chair and they sat down. The host looked discreetly at the guest with his silk stockings, silver buckles on his shoes, black wig and splendid skirt, which had just become fashionable in Paris. And that, he thought, was just the travel habit. What Leibniz saw was poor household goods, a spruce bookcase stood there, a small desk where the

overturning works must have been created. [...] In the next room one could have guessed the machine that grinded the lenses. (Hirsch 2000, p. 99)

This is not the place to go into detail about the philosophical differences between these two great thinkers of the seventeenth century. The stylized presentation, however, shows very nicely the different life circumstances and characters: On the one hand, Spinoza, a Jew of Portuguese origin, who was excommunicated from the Jewish community in Amsterdam in 1656 and who had been cursed, who made his way through life as a lens-grinder, but who was famous and also notorious for his philosophical writings; on the other hand Leibniz, with his philosophical writings not yet published, but sophisticated and already as a young man connected with the big world of international politics and science. Spinoza is a man of principles, who had to endure much hardship for his thinking. His system designs the whole from the one substance. Leibniz, on the other hand, will develop a metaphysics of the plurality of individual substances, and will think of the whole as an interaction of the relations of these individual substances. He himself develops accordingly in a variety of different activities and a network of relationships. The characters and life circumstances could not be more different. Nevertheless, Leibniz has remained for some time in The Hague. There are records of him from that time. One is said to have spoken about the ontological proof of God. The pantheist Spinoza had to react negatively to this. Leibniz solved the problem in an elegant way by noting down the logical proof and giving it to Spinoza in writing.

Court Councillor Leibniz becomes legal advisor and librarian to Duke Johann Friedrich of Brunswick-Lüneburg in Hanover. This Guelph had become Catholic, but he respected the Protestant faith of his subjects and was generally considered a tolerant ruler. The denominational political tolerance of Leibniz thus found fertile ground here. His tasks included not only reforming the state administration, but soon also improving agriculture and manufacturing. Leibniz was supported by the Electress Sophie, the wife of Ernst August, the successor to Johann Friedrich, who died a few years after Leibniz's arrival. Many years later, this close relationship extended to Sophie's daughter, the Electress and later Prussian Queen Sophie Charlotte, with whom Leibniz will be together for months at Charlottenburg Palace near Berlin. Through *the theodicy*, this became a legendary philosophical friendship.

One of the equally legendary events of the first Hanoverian years is the technical project in the Harz Mining. One of the achievements of the inventor Leibniz was the so-called "horizontal wind art", with which he wanted to solve the problem of mine water in the mines of the Harz Mountains. Before the invention of the steam engine, the drainage of the mines was a major obstacle in the development of mining. In the Harz Mountains, a local problem now arose: there was not enough water to operate pumps using water power. However, to use normal wind turbines, such as those used in mills, to drain the mines, the wind was too irregular.

So Leibniz wants to develop a mill that is not vertically in the wind, but consists of wings rotating around a vertical axis (like a gullwing door). Since this horizontal wind art can catch the wind from all sides, it optimizes the utilization of the wind. This wind art has not reached the technical maturity to be actually used. The decisive factor, however, is the rethinking of the concept of technology that underlies Leibniz's experiments:

> All these inventions can be identified by three moments: Firstly, they are often part of entire, sometimes highly

complex *systems*; secondly, they are often aimed at *automation*, i.e. self-control; thirdly, they have a clear *scientific implementation*, since they are not inventions originating in the craft tradition, but are based on highly theoretical considerations of a mathematical, mechanical and hydromechanical nature. (Poser 2016, p. 427)

It is thus important to emphasize the modernity in the thinking of the technician Leibniz: Whereas in Hans Blumenberg (1981), pre-modern technology was about a kind of repetition of nature by other means, that is a still mimetic relationship to nature, modern technology is about *inventio* as an innovative relationship to reality.

Leibniz is versatile in everything he touches. While working on technology in the Harz Mountains, he simultaneously wrote down his considerations on differential calculus, which set the trend for the development of science and were published in the *Acta eruditorum* in 1684 under the title *Nova methodus pro maximis et minimis*. And in everything Leibniz touches, he is innovative. In 1685, the court councillor Leibniz was appointed court historiographer, a milestone in the development of history as a science. It is not only "his immense, everywhere present, admirable polyhistory" (Feuerbach 1984, p. 17) that makes the project of the history of the Guelph House, which accompanied him until the end of his life, an original scientific achievement, but also the turn towards a *methodically* and *source-critically* secured historical science. At that time, it was common to understand historiography as the legitimation of princely claims.

Leibniz does this too on his trip to Italy (which he just undertakes to consult original documents), but in a new, source-critical way. He can trace the Guelphs back to an older lineage, the Estonians. The decisive point here is that the history is not simply a genealogical evidence that legitimizes claims to power, but rather becomes a methodically guided process of research. The function of the court historiographer had a significant political dimension, because *political* claims arose from the *historical* results, so historiography was actually commissioned art. Leibniz, on the other hand, wanted to objectify the procedure scientifically—and thus also make the results independent of political consequences. He proved to be "a very modern thinking scientist who prepared the achievements of the source-critical method of historiography" (Holz 2013, p. 218). He succeeded in this because he "oriented historiography towards the analogy of forensic jurisprudence" (Holz 2013, p. 219), that is towards a procedural objectivity that binds its results to evidence. This source research was the actual reason for the trip to Italy.

The Italian Journey

In his biography of the philosopher, his most trusted colleague Johann Georg Eckhard reproduced an anecdote which Leibniz himself must have passed on orally and which paints an enlightening picture of his character: From Venice, Leibniz boarded a barque on which he was the only traveller. A storm is coming up and the sailors attribute the emerging misfortune to the presence of the heretic (namely Protestant) on board. They decide to throw the thinker overboard without further ado to avert fate. The Protestant Leibniz then takes a rosary from his baggage and soothes the sailors who, at the sight of the person praying the rosary, no longer have the heart to commit their sacrilegious deed. All have gone ashore safely in Mesola.

This story thus testifies "the demonstration of his superior denominational pluralism", and more:

> In the history of religions there is not only the impressive fact of their rigour and martyrs, but also, as a contrast to this, especially in the approach to enlightenment, the impressive fact of those who believe that they can unite in their person all the possibilities of such divisions and fragmentation of man. In it they share the forbearance of their God of reason with the imaginative industriousness of men in their application for his favour. Even this can be done without harming mind and reason, Leibniz shows in the Sea Storm with the rosary in his hand. (Blumenberg 1987, p. 14)

This anecdote depicts a Leibniz who had enough distance in religious matters to be able to use the rite rationally.

Piety and denominational closeness were not his thing. The neighbours in far-away Hanover called him "Glöve nix" (it means "He does not believe in anything" in the local dialect and is an onomatopoeic imitation of his name), because he did not regularly sit with them in church. They were mistaken: he believed in something. It was his faith of reason that made him realize not only that religious customs have a certain function in people's lives, but that they are insignificant for the metaphysical questions of religion, but also that he was tolerant of the plurality of religious rites. That applied with regard to the interdenominational tolerance, for whose promotion he made important contacts on the Italian journey, but also to his intercultural interest, for which he got likewise in Rome decisive impulses. His commitment for China was based on the knowledge from the reports of the Jesuit mission in Beijing, and in the Rites Controversy (i.e., in the question whether Chinese who converted to Christianity were allowed to hold on to their customs or not) Jesuits had spoken out against Dominicans and Franciscans for ritual tolerance, which Leibniz made his own.

Leibniz had come to Venice via southern Germany and a stay in Vienna, leaving the coach and coachman behind to continue his journey by water. The carriage must be mentioned once, because Leibniz spent a lot of time in the carriage during his life, even invented a better suspension for it—probably to be able to write better while driving on the bad roads of that time. The journey went on to Rome and Naples. The "Italian spring, the landscape through which he travelled, the sight of Vesuvius, the art of the Renaissance, the monuments of antiquity, the Italian people and their customs—none of these things can be found in his letters. It was not a German longing for Italy that had brought him here" (Hirsch 2000, p. 233).

In Modena, he proved that the Guelphs were genealogically related to the Este family. In Rome, he met the Jesuit Claudio Filippo Grimaldi, who was about to travel to Beijing. Leibniz had long been very interested in China and had a lively exchange with Grimaldi about the mission in China. For him, it was not only the mission zeal that motivated the Jesuits, but a lively interest in scientific exchange. That was what Leibniz also wanted and then also propagated in his much-read book *Novissima Sinica*. Of course Leibniz as later in his succession also Christian Wolff was interested in Confucian rationalism (Zimmer 2018). In the *Novissima Sinica,* Leibniz himself called China a Europe of the East. Civilization was concentrated at the two ends of Eurasia and would be able to spread in interaction. Again, it makes no sense to accuse Leibniz of Eurocentrism, because, as already mentioned, it was without alternative in the spirit of the epoch. What is important is Leibniz's insight into the power of intercultural exchange, from which everyone should benefit. A more than current thought.

Since Leibniz also pursued his goal of denominational reconciliation diplomatically in Rome, something fundamental should be said at this point: In contrast to Hobbes, who, according to the principle of *bellum omnium contra omnes,* had assumed in political philosophy that claims to freedom would collide, Leibniz "always thought of a reconciliation that should arise from reason and be based on the *common interest* of all those involved. His concept of peace was not one of mutual chessing, but of a well-understood solidarity among people and states" (Holz 2013, p. 224). Leibniz implemented this general irenic concept in his denominational policy—naturally also because religious peace had to be a central demand after the experiences of the past war.

Theoria cum praxi: The Academy Project and the Late Years

The practice of his work in many sciences suggests that Leibniz had an encyclopaedic understanding of science, a notion which will make a career in the eighteenth century Enlightenment philosophy (just think of the famous project of the *Encyclopédie* by Diderot and d'Alembert). Leibniz was always a scientific organizer. In 1700, he reached his goal: his academic society and later Prussian Academy of Sciences was established in Berlin. Leibniz became its first president, and one wrote Leibniz's scientific activity so aptly in his coat of arms: *theoria cum praxi.* The so-called "philosopher king" Frederick II, at whose richly laid table Voltaire will later sit, perhaps mocking Leibnizian optimism on this occasion, called Leibniz "an academy for himself" (Poser 2016, p. 15). As a science politician, he was tireless: he pursued similar academy projects with the emperor in Vienna (where it was only founded much later) and in his advisory activities for Tsar Peter the Great (the foundation of the Russian Academy of Sciences goes back to this suggestion by Leibniz). In all this, the conviction that the promotion of science had to serve the *commune bonum*, the common good, had an effect.

Imagine that: a Court Councillor in Guelphic service in Hanover acts simultaneously as advisor to the Emperor of the Holy Roman Empire *and* the Russian Tsar, who has opened his empire to Europe. This Privy Councillor Leibniz would have liked to have extended his advisory activities to the Emperor of China as well, but this did not happen, either because his letter did not find the long way to the forbidden city or for other unknown reasons. In any case, he thought in dimensions that, with Europe, Russia and China, actually encompassed the whole of Eurasia. It is not surprising that such networking, as we would say today, brought Leibniz not only friends, but also a great deal of mistrust; however, it shows his basic political attitude of wanting to have a balancing, exchanging and promoting effect on science.

This is the political background of his academy program, which he had already designed as a young man in 1669 in the text *Societas Philadelphica* (Leibniz 1966/1967, p. 21 ff.). The scientific organizational background is the encyclopedic breadth of his life's work:

> The detailed research Leibniz pursued covered almost all branches of science of his time. He was one of the leading mathematicians, not only of the seventeenth and eighteenth centuries, but in general; his elaboration of the differential and integral calculus, his geometry of the situation were groundbreaking innovations that could not yet be fully understood and appreciated by his contemporaries, even by outstanding ones like Huygens. But he also distinguished himself as a physicist, he followed biological and medical researches with sympathy, in psychology he was the discoverer of the unconscious. (Holz 2013, p. 187)

Let's take Leibniz's relationship to medicine as a biographically curious example: he had absolutely no confidence in the doctors of his time, because they simply did not yet have the scientific knowledge of the epoch. When he was confronted with diseases in those years around 1700, when he was after all over 50-year-old, he developed "a kind of anamnesis from close self-observation" (Hirsch 2000, p. 316), which he then sent as a report to important doctors of his time. Thus, he not only established the deficient state of the medicine of his time in memoirs and tried to bring it closer to the scientific state of the art beyond weakening permanent bloodletting, but also anticipated, so to speak in a kind of anamnesis procedure in a self-experiment, what scientific medicine today calls differential diagnosis.

Leibniz's outstanding achievements in mathematics, science and technology fall into his early years, he began his historiographical work at the age of 40—but what about philosophy? The philosophical works he *published* himself, in which the system that lies and works behind all his activities becomes visible, is a product of the mature and the late years. Leibniz naturally thought philosophically throughout his life. The first presentation of his philosophy, the *Discours de Métaphysique*, was written in 1686, but was not accessible to contemporaries and the reception of the eighteenth century up to classical German philosophy, as it was not published until the middle of the nineteenth century. This is a problem because, as we will soon see, Leibniz develops in this writing the complete concept of substance that underlies his metaphysics. Leibniz entered the philosophical public in 1695 with the *Système nouveau*. In a nutshell, he develops the development of his metaphysics on the basis of the theory of substance, individual inspired points and pre-stabilized harmony. These are the basic problems of his philosophy.

Furthermore, the extensive works are to be mentioned, of course, although only one was published during his lifetime. Both are biographically related to the philosophical friendship with Sophie Charlotte. She had read John Locke's *Essay Concerning Human Understanding*, and Leibniz wrote his *Nouveaux Essais sur l'entendement humain* between 1701 and 1704 as a response to Locke, but also for the purpose of communicating with the Prussian Queen. The writing discusses the psychology and epistemology of the Englishman against the background of Leibniz's metaphysics and contains his theory of the active mind and *petites perceptions*, which for the first time in the history of philosophy contain a first insight into the unconscious. Leibniz withheld publication because Locke had died in the meantime (also a sign of his considerate and kind treatment of fellow human beings). The work did not appear until 1765, and his unconscious, which was thoroughly rationalistic, came under unilateral reception conditions of Sturm und Drang.

The second extensive work, actually published in 1710 while still alive and which influenced the reception of Leibniz in the first half of the eighteenth century, is the *Essais de theodicée sur la bonté de Dieu, la liberté de l'homme et l'origine du mal*. We will return in detail to this book, which was also motivated by philosophical discussions with Sophie Charlotte. It is an occasional publication, in which Leibniz would like to present the main features of his philosophy to a philosophically interested audience—but also to a lay public in general. This popularization has been further strengthened by the German translation of Gottsched, which appeared after Leibniz's death. If one adds to this the two so-called bequest writings published immediately after his death (the *Principes de la nature et de la grace fondés en raison* of 1718 and the *Monadologie* of 1720), which articulate the model of the *monads* (a term with which Leibniz's philosophy is henceforth identified) in its mature form, one has the corpus of philosophical writings that were available to the early history of reception until the first edition of his works by Dutens in 1768.

It must now be a matter of presenting this philosophy or rather the basic metaphysical model that underlies the whole diversity of his various activities. We have tried to draw a portrait of this *homo universalis* that at least hints at this whole variety, which cannot be developed here in detail and as an overall presentation. But how can we summarize the multifaceted nature of this man? According to the critical edition (www.leibniz-edition.de), we speak of about 100,000 sheets of Leibniz and 15,000 letters in which this richness is presented. Thus his "work resembles a labyrinth through which the way can only be found with a thread of Ariadne's" (Holz 1992, p. 10).

His philosophical gesture is not the academic and systematic philosophy of German idealism, but his mind is scattered throughout the world; yet there is a systematic thought present in the fragments as Ariadne's thread. In the crisis and gradual recovery after the Thirty Years' War, Leibniz becomes visible in the baroque diversity of his interests and fields of activity, and yet also the unity of scientific worldview and metaphysical concept of the world. Leibniz does not have a system spelled out as Wolff and classical German philosophy up to Hegel did after him; but it is a systematic thought that runs through the fragmentary nature of its form of presentation. The unmarried Leibniz was networked with the world, interwoven in his relationships with it—and yet, after he died on November 14, 1716, officially only his secretary and a few strangers stood at his grave.

It is astonishing how precisely and actually still valid today Feuerbach, the first philosopher after the classical history of reception who drew a monographic overall picture, was able to characterize the person Leibniz: "Activity is the essence of his spirit and character" (Feuerbach 1984, p. 23). And furthermore:

> He thought more relative than absolute. We do not have an independent, unrelated, absolute account of his philosophy/ But nevertheless, it is not necessary to resort to a Kantian separation between Leibniz *himself* and Leibniz *for us*. This infinite richness of relationships is the essence of his spirit itself; he is the faithful image of his monad, whose essence is to contain all other beings in an idealistic way, to reflect them in himself, to be in ideal communication and relationship with all things. (Feuerbach 1984, p. 21)

With these words, not only the core of Leibniz's character as a human being is aptly rendered, but also the core of his philosophy: force in the infinite context of the relationships that make up the world in its totality.

Leibniz and the Problem of Metaphysics

The object of our presentation is not an introduction to Leibniz's philosophy in the sense that all the main aspects of his thought are explained in context, so as to give an overview of the whole of this philosophy. Such introductions already exist (Holz 1992; Poser 2005), and it would not make much sense to provide a further overview of the whole of Leibniz's philosophy in addition to these Ariadne's threads, which have been drawn by renowned Leibniz researchers from different approaches through the labyrinth of Leibniz's works. Rather, we want to try to identify a basic metaphysical problem that is perpetuated by the development of Leibniz's thinking and that is present in the various fields of activity that have been outlined so far. It is a matter of identifying a basic idea that has "consequences" for contemporary thought in the sense that it is relevant to the philosophical reflection on the problems of our present day.

Of course, this approach to Leibniz does not only mean interpretation (for even the most comprehensive overall presentation is always an interpretation of its subject), but also a certain association or selection of motifs. Thus, we will concentrate only on the reconstruction of the metaphysical basic idea, and many individual aspects of Leibniz's thought will only be dealt with where they come to the fore in the history of reception itself. On the one hand, this means a certain fragmentation of the philosophical contents (although it does, however, accommodate the gesture of this thinking), but on the other hand, it also means the accentuation of a *systematic* basic idea that runs through and holds together the many aspects, which is just as important for Leibniz. The metaphysical core idea of Leibniz, in the context of modern philosophy, consists in starting from the individuality of the existing and, in particular, of the subject, but to ground it in a concept of the world as a whole that is conceived as a relational unit and interaction of all these individual substances that are involved in their activity. Leibniz thus thinks totality as a unity of the many.

We want to reconstruct this basic problem in the *New System* (simply because it is the first presentation of his philosophy published by Leibniz himself), then in the *Metaphysical Treatise*, we want to catch up on the aspects that remained unknown until the publication of this text in the nineteenth century (above all the complete concept of individual substance), and finally in the late, posthumously published bequest writings (*Principles of Nature* and *Monadology*) to see how this metaphysical concept gets its mature formulation in the concept of the monad.

The continuity of the basic idea is represented by the story of the 15 year-old in Rosental near Leipzig, which old Leibniz tells in his letter to Nicolas Remond from January 10, 1714:

> Already as a child I got to know Aristotle, and even the scholastics did not deter me at all; and even today this does not annoy me at all. But since then Plato and also Plotinus

gave me some satisfaction, without speaking of other old thinkers whom I consulted later. Having outgrown the trivial schools, I fell for the modern, and I remember walking in a grove near Leipzig, called Rosendal, at the age of fifteen to think about whether I should hold on to the substantial forms. [...] Eventually the mechanism got the upper hand and made me study mathematics [...] But when I searched for the last reasons of the mechanism and the laws of motion, I was surprised to see that it was impossible to find them in mathematics, and that one had to return to metaphysics. This led me back to entelechy and from the material to the formal. (W V, 321)

At this point, the whole particularity of Leibniz's approach in the basic constellation of the early modern period in the history of philosophy becomes apparent: in the context of a situation in the history of ideas in which the classical heritage of philosophy and especially of medieval Aristotelism is rejected in the name of the establishment of a mechanical world view and mathematical natural science, the young Leibniz reads precisely those authors who no longer were held in much regard by the epoch—and especially Aristotle, to whom the seventeenth century was particularly distanced, because he was identified with the scholastic dogmatism from which the philosophers of that time wanted to detach themselves. The young Leibniz does not do this in a conservative gesture, not in the sense of a *back to the roots* and not in the sense of acknowledging old authority. But even new authority, which more or less statuary decrees a turning away from the philosophical tradition, does not frighten him to restore the connection to classical thinking from his own thought: for the return to the metaphysics of substantial forms is done from the insight into the limits of mechanical thinking. It must therefore be metaphysically justified. The Rosental story runs like a red thread through the development of Leibniz's thinking. His philosophy is characterized by a unity of scientific worldview and metaphysics.

The New System

With the *Système nouveau*, which first appeared in 1695 in the *Journal des Sçavans* (the oldest scientific journal in Europe) in Paris, Leibniz gave the public a first version of his philosophical system. This already provides a framework for interpretation, since this publication context suggests that Leibniz was concerned with giving profile to his position in the scientific and philosophical context of his time. This, in turn, means that this text is limited to bringing the essential to the point and hiding aspects that might perhaps deepen Leibniz's metaphysical conception, so as not to give rise to misunderstandings. We will see from the example of the great occasional writings such as *Theodicy*, how consciously Leibniz dealt with publication occasions. In any case, the given context makes the *Système nouveau* a particularly suitable testimony to the entry into the world of Leibniz. It is a matter of giving "mechanics as a 'leading science'" (Holz 1992, p. 21) a metaphysical complement to justification—and of delimiting this new method of justification against competing concepts (metaphysics is used in the seventeenth century rationalism essentially to justify the scientific world view): mainly against Descartes, but also against Spinoza.

This is why the concept of substance, which is at the centre of the text and is at the core of Leibniz's metaphysics in general, is particularly suitable for making these differences clear and thus providing the intended delimitation. For Descartes and Spinoza had also formulated their metaphysics via the concept of substance: Descartes, by taking as his starting point the famous two-substance theory, which not only distinguished *res cogitans* and *res extensa*—that is, thinking and extending substance—but also radically separated them in a dualism; and Spinoza, by speaking monistically of the one substance, which could be brought to the one, equally famous formula *Deus sive natura*, that is, pantheistically equating God and nature, in which thinking and expansion then represented two attributes of the one substance.

Leibniz now starts out from a system of *individual* substances, which in their *relationships* form the unity of the whole. In this way, he sets himself apart from the monism of substance in Spinoza, without having to abandon the idea of unity, and with Descartes he can hold on to the subject as point of departure without having to reduce it to a worldless and abstract "I think". Rather, it can be thought in its individuality without separating it from its connection to the world. Leibniz wants to show that the subject, conceived in its individuality, is founded precisely in this world as a whole through its essential relational nature.

Descartes had clearly outlined his concept of substance in the *Discours de la méthode:* he states "that I am a substance whose whole essence or nature consists only in thinking and which does not need a place to be, nor depends on any material thing, so that this I, i.e. the soul through which I am what I am, is completely different from the body" (Descartes 1996, p. 55). In this way, the *cogito*, for which Descartes claims the status of justification, becomes a worldless and placeless "I think", in contrast to which Leibniz represents the unity of body and soul of an I, which always perceives and thinks reality in perspective from one place in the world. The Cartesian experiment of radical doubt poses the question of what remains as an unquestionable thing when all certainties and even the existence of external reality have been questioned. All that remains is the evidence that it is I who think. Consciousness-immanent self-assurance then becomes the unquestionable starting point of well-founded knowledge.

This irrefutable certainty of an unquestionable principle of philosophy, however, has mortgages that must be named in order to be able to measure the scope of Leibniz's alternative model: because Descartes' experiment of radical doubt must also doubt the reality of the world in order to be able to win this principle, he not only gets back a worldless ego, but also a separation of ego and world that can understand everything real exclusively as objectivity set by consciousness. Reality is thus always only given as an *object* of thought and thus as a representational quality—and that is why the correlate of *res cogitans* is then also the *res extensa,* the object of a subject.

More than that, Descartes needs a God to avoid the trap of solipsism that lies in his approach and to restore the mediation of the ego to the world: It is not the objectivity of the world (whose assured scientific knowledge he is actually concerned with) that is necessary, but rather the idea of a God who cannot be a *deus malignus*, a malicious and deceptive God, and thus restore the bridge between the ego and the world.

But since the classicism of the Cartesian approach consists in expressing the two basic concerns of modernity—the foundation of mathematical natural science and the foundation of all world relations from the subject—in a concentrated way in the two-substance theory, Leibniz had to focus primarily on differentiating himself from Descartes in order to give his own answer to these two basic philosophical problems of the epoch. In a short text on the concept of substance, which is in the context of the *New System*,

Leibniz clearly expressed this critical distance to Descartes, which runs through his entire thinking: Although he had "presented some excellent things", he "falsely claimed that the nature of physical substance is in extension, and had no valid concepts of the unity of body and soul, the reason for which was that he did not recognize the nature of substance as a whole" (W I, 197).

It is precisely the problems described here that are at issue in the *New System*, and the fragment on substance does not fail, in recourse to Aristotle and his concept of entelechy, to indicate the essence of substance not seen by Descartes, which is then developed in Leibniz's metaphysics: It is "the concept of *forces*" which "contributes to the knowledge of the true *concept of substance*"; the "ultimate cause of motion in matter" is not to be understood mechanically, but as "an impressed force which is in every body". It is further stated that "this ability to act is in every substance and from it always some kind of effectiveness arises" (W I, 199). Substance is thus not an inert or passive extension, but Leibniz defines it as an active force according to Aristotle's concept of entelechy. This force, which is contained in every individual substance, is the starting point of Leibniz's philosophy, and the interaction of all these substances structures the whole of the universe. Leibniz's metaphysics develops this thought in its aspects and consequences.

Substance as force thus also forms the starting point of the *New System*. Leibniz introduces his remarks with the idea of the complementarity of science and metaphysics. Again it is stated that the physical concept of extended mass must be supplemented by the metaphysical concept of force, because it is "impossible to find *the principles of a true unity* in matter alone or in what is only passive" (W I, 203 f.). In order to articulate this thought, Leibniz introduces the distinction between mathematical and metaphysical points: the former are "the outermost points of the extended", the latter, on the other hand, are points of force, which Leibniz also calls "*soul* points" or substantial forms: "Thus I found that their nature consists in force and that something analogous to feeling and desire results from it and that they must therefore be understood according to the concept we have of *souls*. Aristotle calls them the *first entelechies*, and I call them, perhaps more understandably, *original forces*, which contain not only *reality* (the *act*) or the complementation of possibility, but also an original *effectiveness* (activity)" (W I, 205 f.).

Ultimately, then, the point is (as the reference to Aristotle suggests) to emphasize the difference between dead matter and living being. We will see in more detail later that Leibniz understands this liveliness in its gradual gradation, that is he does not presuppose a fundamental separation of body and soul as Descartes did, but on the contrary assumes its inseparable unity. The ego, however, is the highest level of the living, because it means the reflexive relationship of life to itself: "Beyond this, there is a true unity through the soul or form, which corresponds to what is called the *ego* in us. [...] There are only *substantial atoms*, that is, the real units, completely stripped of parts, which are the sources of the activities and the first absolute principles of the composition of things and, as it were, the last elements of the analysis of substantial things. One could call them *metaphysical points*: they have *something alive*, a kind of *perception*, and the *mathematical points* are their *points of view* for expressing the universe" (W I, 215). Because activity always means action on something, the individual substance with the original force also has its action on others and thus the *relationship to the other within itself*. As perception, the individual substance reflects the effect of others on itself, so that it can be said that every substance is the unity of action and suffering, of active and passive force. The *Système nouveau* calls this "intercourse", that is the reciprocal relationship of each individual substance to all other substances. The essential interrelation of the substance is therefore directly derived from the original force that characterizes it.

The ego is the "true unity" of this context because it consciously reflects it. Moreover, one may assume that Leibniz also emphasizes this ego so prominently in order to place his philosophy emphatically in the context of modernity, which since Descartes has taken the thinking subject as its point of departure—but also to allow the differences to Descartes to emerge clearly. As I said: Leibniz's ego is not a pure *cogito* without a place in the world and without any connection to the body, but on the contrary a reflexive expression of the perception of the universe from a certain place. When Leibniz speaks of the mathematical point as "point of view" of the metaphysical point, he is referring to the fundamental perspectivism that is rooted in his philosophical position.

Every substance reflects the universe from the place in space where it is located and which individuates it: the universe is a multiverse of individual *points de vue*. The title for this unity of the many as a relational unit of all interactions of forces is, in Leibniz's view, the concept of harmony: "The ego, the actual unity, is of an ideal nature and 'reflects' the whole universe in its perceptions. [...] At the same time, however, the universe consists of nothing but the monads, so that both forms of harmony, that of the individual as a unit of perceptions and that of the world as a unit of created substances, are mutually constituted" (Poser 2005, p. 32). Although the concept of the monad does not yet occur in the *New System*, it is, in substance, already anticipated. Also the "unity of body and soul must therefore be thought in a highly complex way as a multiplicity in manifold relations to oneself and to the other individuals" (Poser 2005, p. 33).

Let us now turn to the second aspect, the "intercourse" of substances. At this point, the relationship structure of substances, namely "Descartes had given up the game [...]" (W I, 217). Leibniz is concerned that action and suffering form a unity that lies in the very essence of being in-relation. The individual never *passively* receives something from the outside, but the receiving is always accompanied by the spontaneity of doing. This is what constitutes "their individual character": "For this causes that, since each of these substances expresses the whole universe precisely in its own way and according to a certain point of view", each of them "exists as in a world of its own" (W I, 219). Later Leibniz will call this the so often misunderstood "windowlessness" of the monad. It essentially means already at this point the unity of the individual interaction of each substance; it is an expression of its relationship to the whole and perspective on the whole.

Spontaneity in the context of relationships, the unity of autonomy in and dependence on the whole is thus what constitutes the individuality of the many who make up the whole. This is the problem of metaphysics as it is for Leibniz. The relationship is immanent in substance, and in this thought the circle of the complementary unity of natural science and metaphysics closes. Nothing can mathematically determine "absolute motion [...] because everything is defined by relations" (W I, 225). This is the basic idea of Leibniz' physical dynamics, but also of his metaphysics: it is the

> mutual relationship regulated from the outset in every substance of the world, which produces what we call their *intercourse*, and which is the only *connection between soul and*

body. [...] This hypothesis is possible. For why should God not a priori be able to give the substance a nature or inner force that would produce in it, according to an order (as in a *spiritual or formal automaton, but free* in that part of which is reason), whatever happens to it. (W I, 221)

This quotation expresses *in a nutshell* the basic idea of the Leibniz system: interacting *inner* forces, which in their unit of relationship form an *ordering structure* that we can call totality. We must pursue this idea further: first its development in the main metaphysical writings, then its fate in the history of reception, and finally its significance for political philosophy.

Discours de Métaphysique: The Complete Concept of Individual Substance

About 10 years before the *Système nouveau,* Leibniz had written down the first coherent account of his philosophy in 1686 in the *Discours de Métaphysique.* This writing was, as mentioned, published posthumously only in the nineteenth century and was thus unknown to the entire reception from the Enlightenment to Hegel. This is a particular pity because this text contains the complete concept of substance by Leibniz, which will then find its final and mature form in the late bequest writings in the concept of the monad. We shall now go back to this first document of Leibniz's systematic thinking in order to identify elements which, compared with the diction in the *New System,* which is very much directed towards clarity of presentation, expose additional aspects which can then lead to the mature form of the system.

The reason for writing the *discourse* was Leibniz's discussion with the philosopher Antoine Arnauld, who belongs to the theological school of Jansenism. The background is Leibniz's denominational political intention to prepare for a reunification of the Christian denominations. He wants to give Arnauld an outline of his metaphysical position with the *Discourse* in order to prepare the discussion. For a thorough and detailed interpretation of the text, which cannot be our intention here, the extensive correspondence between Leibniz and Arnauld would have to be consulted. For our purpose, the reconstruction of the concept of substance and its implications, this aspect can be neglected.

After all, one should have the background of the origin in mind, because it essentially determines the course of argumentation. The *discourse* does not begin like the *Système nouveau* with the concept of substance, but with the concept of God. This use is of course essential for the argumentation towards Arnauld, but for our context the first seven paragraphs can be left out. For in order to expose the philosophical-systematic core of the text, the argumentation must be detached from the theological context. This does not mean that this dimension does not exist or that it is unimportant, but that it is not essential for the reconstruction of the concept of substance. We will return to the *philosophical* concept of God, which is independent of theological considerations, in the context of the later bequest writings.

The *concept of individual substance* is introduced to clarify the difference between divine and creaturely action. However, in order to provide this clarification, one must know "what such a substance is". And this is where the completely new definition that Leibniz gives to the concept of substance comes into being:

One must therefore consider what is truly attributed to a particular subject. Now it is certain that every true proposition has a basis in the nature of things, and if a proposition is not identical, that is, if the predicate is not expressly contained in the subject, it must be virtually contained in it, and this is what philosophers call *in-esse* (being in) by saying that the predicate *is in the* subject. Thus, the concept of the subject must always include that of the predicate, in such a way that the one who fully understands the concept of the subject would also judge that the predicate belongs to it. Since this is so, we can say that the nature of an individual substance or a complete being is to have a concept so fulfilled that it is sufficient to understand all the predicates of the subject to which that concept is attributed and to derive them from it. (W I, 75)

At this point it may be misleading at first that Leibniz presents his thought in the form of a logical proposition (*praedicatum inest subiecto*). Such a logical theory does indeed exist in Leibniz, but the formula is introduced here not as a logical but as an ontological determination—for Leibniz speaks of the determination of the essence of individual substance and its subject character. Substance is, according to its Aristotelian basic determination, a carrier of properties (logically speaking: "underlying", i.e., *subiectum*, to which predicates belong). Now one could see that Leibniz determined substance from the concept of force, that is as an action that produces its determinations from itself. There are properties which are not yet explicitly (i.e., actually realized), but which are very much "virtual", that is possibly in the subject. The "being in" of the predicates then means, in an ontologically strict sense, that the subject always already contains everything that is real and possible as a unity in itself, because as a force it is the reason for this unity of reality and possibility.

The complete concept of individual substance is thus the unfinished and also unfinishable whole of the subject's real and possible being: a borderline concept for perfection, whereby, in order to avoid misunderstandings, it must be said that Leibniz always understood by this a degree of perfection, that is ultimately an increase in one's own reality. In other words: "The individual is characterized by his *complete concept of individual substance*. This term 'includes all its past, present and future predicates'" (Poser 2005, p. 125).

Now the individual substance is also an in-being in the sense that it stands in the world and its relational context. In this respect, the logical formula *praedicatum inest subiecto* in the ontological transmission of *discourse* also means the thesis of universal mediation of the individual with the whole. Each individual expresses the whole, because on the one hand the subject is in the world (contained in it), on the other hand the world is contained in each individual substance by representing and expressing it from its perspective. The whole is not given in any other way than in the perspective representation, the *repraesentatio mundi* as expression of the whole in each of its individual parts.

This connection, that "*each individual substance expresses the whole universe in its own way*" (W I, 77), as it is stated in the summary Leibniz wrote for Arnauld, is clarified by the continuation of the argumentation: for the given structure means that the place of expression of the whole individuates the substance and "it is not true that two substances are completely identical and *solo numero* (in number alone) different". And then, in order to make this connection evident, Leibniz introduces the mirror metaphor: "Moreover, each substance is like a whole world and like a mirror of God, or rather of the whole universe, each of which expresses itself in its own way, just as one and the same city presents itself according to the different locations of the one who looks at it. Thus, in a certain way, the universe is multiplied as often as there are substances" (W I, 77f.).

The mirror metaphor is further elaborated in the later writings, namely in the concept of the monad as a living mirror (we will come back to this). At this point, the metaphor of the city, which one looks at from different locations, contours Leibniz's *perspectivism*, which is strictly metaphysical and arises from the basic ontological concept: each individual reflects the whole from its location in the world—and thus represents a unique and unmistakable view of it. However, perspectivism also includes another aspect of being in, which leads to a new concept of the world and a completely new understanding of totality. In principle, the world as a whole is never given *as if it is seen from outside as a whole* (this would indeed be bad metaphysics, which Kant rightly criticized). It is always only given from an inner-worldly perspective, that is it is an expression of the whole, but only in perspective refraction. Totality then becomes a transempirical, that is not given in experience, but not contradicting it either, concept of the whole as a unity of all inner-worldly interactions of these perspective forms of expression.

This leads Leibniz to the beautiful formulation, "that every substance is, as it were, a world of its own" (W I, 95). It is the perspective that makes it individual: "Although all express the same phenomena, their contents are not completely equal, but it is enough that they are proportional; as when several viewers believe they see the same thing and understand each other, although each speaks in his own way according to his perspective" (W I, 95). This is, in contrast to the solipsism of the pure *cogito* in Descartes, a position that accentuates the many perspectives in a *common* and *shared* world: for in the concept of perspective there is that *many* refer to *one thing*. Plurality is not to be confused with the arbitrariness of pluralism: Leibniz formulates very clearly "that what is special for some is common to all. Otherwise there would be no connection" (W I, 97). But it is precisely this substantial *connection* of the many and not their atomistic dispersion that Leibniz' metaphysics is concerned with.

A further motif, which is more pointedly executed in comparison to the *New System* in *Discourse*, is the essential unity of action and suffering. This aspect will be dealt with in detail in the context of a political theory of compossibility and its consequences at the end of this book. Leibniz states that "the substances hinder or limit each other, and in this sense one can say that they interact and are, so to speak, forced to adapt to each other. For it can happen that a change which increases the content of expression of one person reduces that of another" (W I, 101). This entanglement of action and suffering is a metaphysical basic idea of Leibniz, which necessarily results from the two basic statements about individual substance, namely its determination as force and as being in relationship.

Josef König put this basic idea in the following very apt words: "The difference between doing and suffering has its metaphysical origin in doing itself" (König 1978, p. 38). This is because substances are limited by the fact that they are all more or less active. Action is the cause of suffering; autonomy and dependence form an indissoluble link characterized by the fact that everything is somehow related to everything else. By acting, developing and realizing ourselves, we necessarily restrict other development. In the same sense, however, the actions of others have a limiting effect on me. Freedom and dependence are two sides of the same coin—this basic metaphysical insight of Leibniz will lead him to the concept of compossibility, not in a logical sense (two propositions are compossible, i.e. they are possible at the same time, if they do not contradict each other), but as an ontological definition: if all individual substances are essentially characterized by the fact that they act and act in relation to each other, then action must, as far as possible, be designed in such a way that they do not exclude each other, but can act and develop at the same time. From a metaphysical insight arises the political-normative demand to create an order that allows as many possibilities for development as possible at the same time. We will come back to this.

Leibniz made the connection to the problem of freedom itself explicit:

> Thus God alone creates the connection or communication of the substances, and it is through them that the phenomena of the one meet and coincide with those of the other, and that consequently there is something real in our perceptions. [...] We also see that every substance has a perfect spontaneity (which in intelligent substances becomes freedom), that everything that happens to it is a consequence of its idea or its being, and that nothing determines it except God alone. (W I, 151)

The *problem of metaphysics* is the *justification of this freedom*, however not in an abstract sense, but as a well-founded freedom in the order context of the whole. This constitutes the connection between metaphysics and politics, which will be examined in more detail in the last chapter.

The Concept of the Monad

In the Late Writings, Leibniz summarizes all the provisions we have reconstructed so far in the term for which he has become famous: the concept of the monad. Here, the metaphysical basic ideas take on their final and mature form. Leibniz first carries out this identification of substance and monad in *Principes de la nature et de la grâce, fondés en raison*: "*Substance* is a being capable of action. It is simple or compound. The *simple substance* is that which has no parts. The *compound substance* is the accumulation of simple substances or *monads*. *Monas* is a Greek word meaning unity or that which is one" (W I, 415).

In contrast to the previous writings, Leibniz uses the term monad to accentuate the aspect of unity, in such a way that this unity is sought precisely in the smallest, indivisible, irreducible, and not in the whole, which is rather understood as composed of these smallest units. The unit of the whole or totality is the relational unit of the interactions of these monads as the actual units of which the universe is composed. It is through this principled composition of the whole of nature that the idea arises through which Leibniz distinguishes himself from Descartes' dualistic world view: Nature does not make any leaps, everything in it is gradually built up in stages, because it was originally composed. Thus, the spirit is not *separated* from nature, but is interpreted as its reflexive expression: "The beings in whom such conclusions cannot be ascertained are called *animals*; but those who know these necessary truths are, in the true sense, those who are called *beings of reason*, and their souls are called *spirits*. These souls are capable of performing reflective acts" (W I, 423).

Also in the *principles,* it is the actions that individualize the monads: "In nature, everything is filled up. There are everywhere simple substances which are indeed separated from each other by their own actions and which constantly change their relationships with each other" (W I, 417). One can see that the basic idea of the individual substance, to be a unity of action and suffering in one relationship, persists. Leibniz now calls this in the *Principles* and also in the *Monadology* perception and *striving*, and also speaks directly of "relationships" instead of "intercourse". However, these are conceptual clarifications of one and the same basic idea, which Leibniz now puts into a likewise very precise metaphor for this whole of the structural unit of monads. He expresses it in the image of the *living mirror,* namely "that every monad is a living mirror or is endowed with inner action, that it represents the universe according to its point of view and is regulated in the same way as the universe itself" (W I, 417).

What does this talk about the living mirror mean? The meaning of the metaphorical license of the mirror's *liveliness* (because mirrors are actually not living things) is indicated by the quote itself: it consists in the monad's inner action. But what *structure* does the talk of the mirror actually refer to? It expresses a relationship of being: A mirror is a being, a thing among other things, which, however, is characterized by *carrying within itself* an image of the other thing. This means that the mirror contains an image of its relationship to the other, and this image expresses the relationship by *showing* or *making visible* the character or structural peculiarity of this relationship of being. The mirroring expresses the *perspective of the virtual image*, because each mirror reflects its other from the place and therefore from the perspective in which it stands as a whole.

In this respect, Leibniz's talk of the mirror is a very precise metaphor for the whole of his basic idea: the monad *contains* the whole in the manner of a picture that expresses its relationship to the whole in perspective. This is also the meaning of the monad's famous "windowlessness": the reflection does not mean the doubling of an externally "incoming" reality in the mirror image, but rather the perspectival reflection of this reality from a place and—here the relevance of the liveliness of the reflection arises—through a focus on this reality. In *Monadology*, the metaphor of the living mirror is accentuated for its metaphysical consequence, namely that the basic idea expressed in it implies a universal mediating connection of all with all: "This connection now, or this adaptation of all created things to each of them and of each individual to all others, has the effect that every simple substance enters into relations that express all others and that it is consequently a permanent living mirror of the universe" (W I, 465).

Monadology reiterates this concept of the monad and adds this very image of windowlessness to the mirror metaphor introduced to shed light on the monadic *structure* of the world as a whole: "The monads have no windows through which anything can enter or exit them. [...] Thus neither substance nor accidental external influences can enter a monad" (W I, 441). It carries, as already developed, not only everything that it is within itself, but also everything that happens to it: for both result from its own active striving and action on others and are thus the result of the relationships to which the monad gives structure through its own action. In other words: "The individual being is what it is, only in that the whole of the world is the necessary and sufficient condition of its individual being. [...] The individual has always been the manifestation of the whole. Consequently, there is no need for a window to relate the other to the substance, for it *is* itself this other, albeit in mirror image" (Holz 1992, p. 113). With the windowlessness of the monad, Leibniz wants to say that it is not determined by anything individual and isolatable that affects it from the outside, but always by the interaction with the whole. The monad is a windowless expression of this whole in the interplay of its effect on the context from its individual location and its thereby co-determined effect through this context. This means that the monad is always already in connection and therefore windowless, because it does not have to get in connection first.

A truly new element of monadology compared to the metaphysical main and program writings discussed so far is the doctrine of principles developed at the end of this paper. It should be noted that *Monadology* must be regarded as the philosophical testament of Leibniz. Almost like a telegram he summarizes the basic principles of his philosophy. Ortega y Gasset has identified a list of ten principles in his Leibniz book (1966/1967, p. 14 f.). *Monadology* merely states the central principles of Leibniz's rationalism: the principle of contradiction and sufficient reason, and further equally fundamental basic principles of his metaphysics, namely the distinction between factual truths and rational truths and the principle of the best (W I, 453 ff.). If one adds the ontological (i.e., the philosophically and not theologically founded) concept of God and the idea of universal harmony, which are addressed at the end of the text, one has the core statements of Leibniz's philosophy together.

The principle of contradiction is a resumption of the basic idea of the Aristotelian principle of the excluded middle. In order to be able to think something, we have to hold on to this something as identity (A=A). Since one could not think without this principle, and thus could not prove anything, it is a basic principle that is itself unprovable (as, by the way, is the evidence of the variety's experience, namely that manifold things are perceived by me). Both principles, namely that only identical things can be true and that a plurality of phenomena is perceived by me (*varia a me percipiuntur*), are themselves unprovable prerequisites of rational thinking. Without them knowledge is not possible. Also the principle of sufficient reason—*nihil sine ratione*—aims at the foundation of the rationalist world view of philosophy: For a reasonable concept of reality it must be assumed that nothing in the world happens without a reason, that is that potentially everything is *explainable*. Without this precondition, it would be absurd to search for explanations and to justify purposes. This does not mean that we know everything, but that basically everything is open to knowledge: The fact that "reasons often cannot be known to us" (W I, 453) does not mean for Leibniz that there are things we cannot know, but rather describes the open horizon of the process of knowledge.

The distinction between necessary truths of reason, which can be deductively understood, and contingent factual truths, which arise a posteriori from experience, is an essential insight of Leibniz's thinking: "Truths of reason are necessary and their opposite is impossible, and factual truths are contingent and their opposite is possible" (W I, 453). Here, Leibniz occupies a middle position between the rationalism of Descartes, which only recognizes truths of reason, and British empiricism, which only accepts empirical findings. To combine both forms of knowledge into a well-defined unit (i.e., to distinguish them, but not to separate them as mutually exclusive alternatives) is a trend-setting merit of Leibniz's metaphysics.

Finally, the principle of the best, which will continue to occupy us both in the context of the theodicy problem and in the question of the topicality of Leibniz' political thought in the concept of compossibility. This principle states that in the interplay of the forces represented by the monads, the constellation of realizations and thus the reality that allows more realization (in Leibniz' terminology: more perfection) always prevails. Force is possibility, which pushes towards reality. Since all monads are characterized by their striving (and we have seen that acting always means suffering at the same time), reality is always the reality of the simultaneously possible. For if action means suffering, that is limited other action, suffering is defined as an unrealized possibility to act.

If you think the principle of sufficient reason to its logical conclusion, then you need a final reason that holds the nexus of reasons together. When Leibniz speaks strictly philosophically, then God means the final reason: "Thus the final reason of things must lie in a necessary substance in which the particular of changes occurs only in an eminent way as in the source, and this substance we call *God*. [...] One can also judge that this supreme substance, which is unique, universal and necessary, which has nothing but itself that is independent of it and which is a simple consequence of its possibility, is such that it cannot have any limits and contains as much reality as is possible" (W I, 457). Beyond theological determinations and also considerations God is strictly metaphysically speaking "an infinitesimal limit function" (Holz 1992, p. 75) for the world as a whole.

The universal ultimate reason of which Leibniz speaks (and of which he says that we *call* it "God") is thus synonymous with the structural whole of totality: for not only God but also the world itself as a whole can be thought in such a way that it has nothing independent of its being except for it, and is in its reality the "consequence of its possibility": "Because there is nothing else except it, the unconditional being can be only one; only one thing is unconditional, namely the world in its entirety" (Holz 1992, p. 77). The point is that Leibniz, unlike Spinoza, does not claim pantheism, that is metaphysically speaking not the identity of God and nature, but makes clear that one can theologically and philosophically *speak* of God— but if he is *philosophically* conceived as "ultimate reason", then the content of meaning is ontologically synonymous with the defining features of the world as a whole. And that in turn means: I *can* think the metaphysical model of Leibniz also without God.

Irrespective of whether this whole is *called* God or not, Leibniz is concerned with a structural whole of the connection of the many, which he calls "universal harmony": namely, "that every substance expresses exactly all the others through the relations that exist in it", in order to "maintain as much diversity as possible, but in connection with the greatest possible order" (W I, 465). Those who like can call this order God. But this is not necessary, for it can also only designate the structure of the relational unit of the world as a whole.

Leibniz summarized the basic philosophical idea that we reconstructed in an unsent supplement to his letter to Remond of July 1714. It is a short presentation of his metaphysics, which shows very nicely Leibniz's ability to adapt his speech to the respective addressee. All essential aspects of his philosophy are addressed in clear words:

> I believe that the whole universe of creatures consists only of simple substances or monads and associations of them. These simple substances are what in us and in the genii is called spirit and in the animals soul. They all have perception (which is nothing other than the representation of multiplicity in unity) and appetite (which is nothing other than the striving from one perception to another), which in animals is called *drive* and where perception is understanding, *will*. Other than this could not be thought of at all in simple substances and, consequently, in all nature. The associations are what we call bodies. In this mass, matter or suffering force or original resistance is what is called passivity in the bodies and what is considered the same everywhere. But the active primal force is what we can call entelechy, and in that the mass is different. However, all these bodies and everything that is attributed to them are not substances, but only well-founded phenomena, which are different in different

observers, but which are related to each other and come from one and the same basis, comparable to the different phenomena of one and the same city, which is viewed from different sides. Space, far from being substance, is not even a being. Like time, it is an order, an order of what exists together, just as time is an order among existences that are not at the same time. (W V, 335 f.)

Leibniz Reception from the Enlightenment to Hegel

In the middle of the eighteenth century, there was an event that not only shook the earth, but also deeply shook many of the human beliefs that had been valid until then. Goethe described this in his autobiography *Poetry and Truth*: "However, an extraordinary world event shook the boy's composure for the first time in the deepest way. On the first of November 1755 the earthquake in Lisbon occurred, and spread a tremendous horror over the world already inhabited in peace and quiet" (Goethe 1981a, p. 29). This earthquake not only reduced Lisbon to rubble, but also shattered the optimism of the era. The "inhabited" world of peace was the century after the end of the Thirty Years' War, and one could rightly add: the century of Leibniz. The first part of this period between the middle of the seventeenth and the middle of the eighteenth century was shaped by himself, and the first decades of the eighteenth century were marked by the Early Enlightenment, which in terms of reception had a positive attitude towards the works known at that time.

The Lisbon earthquake, however, destroyed this trust in God and Providence, and Goethe very impressively clothed the awakening of the era from its naive faith in the doubts of the young man who had been himself:

> The boy who had to hear all this repeatedly was not a little affected. God, the Creator and Sustainer of heaven and earth, whom the explanation of the first article of faith so wisely and graciously presented to him, had by no means proved Himself fatherly by abandoning the righteous to the same perdition as the unrighteous. In vain did the young mind seek to establish itself against these impressions, which was all the less possible because the wise and the scribes themselves could not unite over the way in which such a phenomenon should be viewed. (Goethe 1981a, p. 30 f.)

The earthquake was a watershed of the century in terms of mental history, and it was certainly also a crossroads in the reception of Leibniz. For it was in the context of the event that probably the most famous criticism of Leibniz arose, which Voltaire satirically presented in his novel *Candide or Optimism*. The novel describes how the philosopher Pangloss, despite all his suffering and bad experiences, steadfastly adheres to his metaphysical principles: "Pangloss taught metaphysico-theologico-cosmology. He proved in an excellent way that there is no effect without cause, that in this best of all worlds the Baron's castle is the most beautiful of all castles and the Baroness the best of all baronesses" (Voltaire 1972, p. 10f.). And Candide, the faithful pupil, after a series of bad experiences with the world, defines optimism as "the madness of claiming that everything is good, even when one is feeling bad" (Voltaire 1972, p. 105). But Pangloss still clings to Leibniz in the galley: "[T]he fact is that I am a philosopher, and it is therefore impossible for me to retract my words, all the less so because Leibniz cannot be wrong and there is nothing more beautiful in the world than pre-stabilized harmony, filled space and immaterial substance" (Voltaire 1972, p. 173f.). No friendly words about Leibniz, and no friendly look at the philosophers. But from Voltaire to Kant the critical voices about Leibniz are increasing, even if they are not the only ones.

The Theodicy Problem

Voltaires' mockery refers to the *Theodicy of the goodness of God, the freedom of man and the origin of evil*, and it need not be emphasized that it does not do justice to the ideas set forth in this extensive work. Leibniz is concerned with the possibility of the conformity of faith with reason, a problem which the first treatise discusses in extensive discussions. If one looks at *Theodicy* from a problem-based perspective, that is with the question of the topicality of the problem articulated here for the present time, this aspect certainly does not belong any longer to our philosophical basic questions, but was however quite important for the context of the work's origin. On the one hand, a reasoning of faith on grounds of reason could have a balancing effect in denominational conflicts, on the other hand it was necessary to make faith and reason compatible in the emerging age of Enlightenment.

Today, in a time when faith and knowledge can be clearly distinguished, this is of course an obsolete question. But historically, in the early Enlightenment, after its publication in 1710 and its popularization through Gottsched's translation into German, this writing became so tremendously effective until the middle of the century because it showed that the world of the Bible did not have to contradict the new, scientific worldview. And it was also a matter of using the means of speculative philosophy to show why God could only choose the best of all possible worlds. Here, we have a question that as an ontological problem beyond the theological horizon of the epoch is still relevant for our thinking today.

Right at the beginning of the preface Leibniz makes clear what he is concerned with: "At all times the masses of people have seen the worship of God as consisting of formalities: *true piety*, i.e. enlightenment and virtue, has never been an inheritance of the great number. Just as true piety consists in attitude and practical action, so, accordingly, the *formalities of devotion* are twofold; some amount to *ceremonial acts*, others to *dogmas*" (W II.1, 3). Leibniz's intention, made explicit here in his opening statement, is to replace ritual and dogmatic religiosity (to which, as we have already seen, he was very tolerant) with moral conviction and action for reasons. This then made *theodicy* the "Bibel der Aufgeklärten (Bible of the Enlightened)" (Hirsch 2000, p. 463).

Here, as in his ethical writings in general, he is concerned with the moral perfection of man. This basic direction becomes clear when one realizes that the theodicy problem *ontologically* puts the question about the modalities (relationship of reality, possibility and necessity) and ethically the problem of freedom into the centre of the reflection. In the core it is not, as Voltaire thought, about justifying evil, but about the problem that theologically speaking God and philosophically speaking the ontological theory of the theodicy must *allow* evil in order not to give up the concept of freedom. Basically, Leibniz defends the idea of human freedom in the *Theodicy*—and that too makes this work a 'Bible' of the early Enlightenment in Germany.

To summarize the argument: Cynical in the sense of Voltaire's criticism is the distinction that God did not want evil but only allowed it, only if one disregards the central question of man's freedom. This is an old problem—already Augustine insisted on freedom of will, because without it there can be no sin, and without sin there can be no necessity of salvation. But that is no longer Leibniz's problem. For him it is not about redemption but about the foundation of human freedom: about "entering the space of faith with philosophical categories and reversing the relationship between philosophy and theology. That theodicy becomes a problem shows that a maid of theology has become a reason that is right with faith" (Poser 2016, p. 45). And this freedom implies ontologically, that is from philosophical premises, a space of possibility, which then must also contain the possibility of evil.

Working through the many hundreds of pages of this text may only make sense for experts today. Whoever does it nevertheless discovers a detailed knowledge of scholastic theories that is unusual for the period, and thus sees that the intuition of the young Leibniz in the Rosental, not to simply push aside the traditional problems of philosophy, still works for the old Leibniz. And whoever reads can see a distinction at work, which is in any case still relevant: *the theodicy* is written for the philosophical understanding with Sophie Charlotte and as a published work for a broad public, but not for the philosophical experts. Leibniz, however, claims to be able to strictly metaphysically reformulate and justify this, so to speak, exoteric form of presentation at any time.

He thus adapts his presentation to his addressee: "In fact, the mode of presentation is a problem that runs through Leibniz's entire oeuvre. Where he writes for a correspondent, he sometimes takes his way of thinking into account to such an extent that his own position is only discernible through a tinted glass. Leibniz himself has emphasized that he tries to formulate 'exoterically' for the audience's understanding of what must be said differently in 'acroamatic' rigour (or *à la rigueur métaphysique*)" (Holz 2015, p. 45). Here, a methodological awareness as a philosophical writer is evident which is still exemplary today: because if we do not want to remain in the ivory tower of philosophical experts among ourselves, but if philosophy is to have an effect in the public sphere and make a practical difference, then we still face the problem of having to formulate philosophical theories and statements in such a way that a general public can understand them. Leibniz' demand for retranslatability into metaphysical rigour (and thus into philosophical contexts of justification), however, requires that such a generally understandable presentation must not be at the price of theoretical inconsistency. A highly interesting "side issue" of *theodicy*.

If we look for a philosophical Ariadne's thread that can show us a way (and that does not mean: the way) through the extensive labyrinth of thoughts of *Theodicy*, we can take up the problem of modalities and, connected with it, the problem of freedom. This also has the advantage of opening up a philosophically more precise interpretation of the speech of the best of all possible worlds. Already in the preface this concern of Leibniz about a "misunderstood necessity" becomes clear when he distinguishes between "*fatum mahumetanum,* fate according to the Turkish view", which assumes that we have no influence on the course of things, and "*fatum stoicum*", which "did not distract people [...] from the concern for their affairs" (W II.1, 17).

Leibniz is thus concerned quite centrally with freedom as the responsibility of man for his own affairs. He argues ethically and in terms of modal ontology: so "one can also realize the strange consequences of a fateful necessity in another way, if one considers that it would abolish the freedom of the will, which is nevertheless essential for the morality of action" (W II.1, 23). It is a matter of "showing degrees of necessity" (W II.1, 25), in order to establish margins of freedom. To act freely means not to be conditioned or only partially conditioned from outside. If we have learned from the description of Leibniz's philosophy that forces are in relationships and thus dependencies and conditions, then the degrees of necessity are degrees of determinacy, which limits, but does not absolutely negate, the scope of freedom. Consequently, free action means to realize possibilities, and therefore freedom theory is always bound to the problem of modalities: "Possibility, reality and necessity must therefore be delimited and related to each other in *every* theory of freedom" (Poser 2016, p. 220).

In the preface, there is also the famous formula about the best of all possible worlds, which is also thought from the modal problem and which we must understand in terms of modal ontology in detail: Namely "that God chose the most perfect of all possible worlds and was determined by his wisdom to admit the evil associated with it" does not mean a justification of the best world, but only means that "this world is all in all the best that could be chosen" (W II.1, 53). Ontologically speaking: it is not the *best* but the best of the *possible* worlds, because only this world and no other possible world *could* become reality. Leibniz calls this insight, as we have seen in the presentation of his philosophy, the "*principle of the best*". The reality of *this* world is always the result of the interaction of all interacting forces—and therefore not the *best* of all, but the best of all *possible* worlds.

And so the evil has beyond the theological discourse also an ontological sense. In the overall context of the interactions of forces "action and suffering are always reciprocal among creatures" (W II.1, 305). And that means: if we want to think of a concept of world that by the conditional context of being in relationship of everything with everything opens a space of possibility and with it of freedom, we must accept evil, since in this infinite context as finite we not only do something but always suffer something. Leibniz himself addresses this systematic background to the metaphysical concept of force and entelechy (W II.1, 335), and we have already seen that active and passive force form an irrevocable unity in Leibniz' metaphysical model. And in this context, we must accept that contingency is a precondition of freedom:

> I have shown that the freedom that one wants to have in the schools of theologians consists in *insight*, which includes a precise knowledge of the object of contemplation, in the *spontaneity* with which we decide, and finally in *randomness*, that is, in the exclusion of logical or metaphysical necessity. Insight is as it were the soul of freedom, but the rest is only as it were the body and the basis. (W II.2, 75)

In Leibniz's thinking, there is a very differentiated concept of freedom, which will occupy us even further. It is not about the formal and abstract concept of freedom of the political philosophy of his time and of the bourgeois age in general, but about placing spontaneity and insight in the context of their conditions, that is also thinking freedom and dependence together. With it the concept of freedom stands in the context of the ontological concept of compossibility, which gives only its full ontological meaning to the formula about the best of the possible worlds. One must not reduce compossibility to a merely logical category. The term also has this logical sense with Leibniz: propositions are logically possible at the same time, that is they are simultaneously possible, if they do not contradict each other.

As an ontological category, however, compossibility aims at a concept of the real, which understands reality as a unity of the simultaneously possible: "All possible strives for realisation because it is possible. For reality is the state that is possible for the possible. Being in-possibility carries within itself the tendency to become real. Since Aristotle, this has been a common thought in philosophy, which Leibniz, the great philosopher of possibility, has matured. Now, however, in an infinite world there are in principle infinite possibilities, many of which are mutually exclusive. At the same time, only that which is possible together, which is compossible, can become real" (Holz 2013, p. 119).

That Leibniz wanted compossibility to be understood as an *ontological principle* is something he himself expressed in the sentence *Omne possibile exigit existere:*

> *The absolutely first truths* are, among the identical truths of reason and among the factual truths, those from which all experience can be proved a priori, namely: *all possible things strive for existence* and therefore exist, unless something else, which also strives for existence, prevents it and is incompatible with the former, from which follows that always that connection of things exists in which most exists. (W I, 177)

This is the full meaning of Leibniz's formula of the best of all possible worlds: it is the optimal order of what is simultaneously possible.

Only such possibilities can become real, which are compatible. If everything possible urges for realization and some possibilities exclude others from realization, because otherwise everything possible would become reality and would then no longer be a possibility, then world in its reality always means the highest possible degree of realization of possibility, that is, the highest possible degree of reality that Leibniz calls perfection. The best world is the one that makes the greatest number of simultaneous realizations possible: a concept of world that will still have to be investigated in its significance for the present, that is, how the world is to be thought today. Only this much is clear: the philosophical content of *Theodicy*, which goes far beyond the theological horizon of its historical background, is not even seen, let alone met by Voltaire's sharp mocking criticism.

Transformations in the Enlightenment: Wolff and Baumgarten

The beautiful definition that Christian Wolff has given philosophy as the *science of the possible* makes him seemingly already a Leibnizian. However, the question remains here as in the whole of his reception of Leibniz, whether Wolff really does justice to the degree of differentiation of the 'metaphysician of possibility' Leibniz. In any case, the judgment heard from Kant to Hegel, which reduces Wolff to a mere dogmatic school philosopher, is unfair. In the lifetime of this man, there has been a thrust of scientific progress at German universities, in which he himself has been involved in a very commendable way. He played a major part in the formation of a German national culture in the eighteenth century by presenting his philosophy in his mother tongue, thus becoming the creator of German philosophical terminology.

This too is a process that Leibniz had suggested: "It is well known that language is a mirror of understanding, and that the people, when they uplift the intellect, also at the same time well practice the language that the Greeks, Romans and Arabs show in their examples" (Leibniz 1968, p. 45). Leibniz' German, somewhat awkward compared to the polished Latin and elegant French known from him, seems to almost testify to the need for reform of the mother tongue, and he has explicitly called for this necessity of establishing German as the language of philosophy: "There is, however, a certain loss of our language in those things which one can neither see nor feel [...]; in which even more subtracted and cunning explanations, as the lovers of wisdom in their way of thinking, and in the general teaching of things under the name of logic and metaphysics bring things on track" (Leibniz 1968, p. 46). In other words: Germans must learn to express abstract facts appropriately in their mother tongue.

Wolff carried out this program in the whole systematic breadth of philosophy. Between 1712 and 1723, *Reasonable thoughts* was produced on all the then essential areas of philosophy, from logic and metaphysics to ethics, physics and teleology. It was only after Wolff had published this impressive series of German writings that he set about the Latin work, which then helped him to European fame. All in all, it can be said that he thus gave all the disciplines of philosophy their philosophical vocabulary in German, and did so on the basis of the demand for strictly derived, precise concepts, methodically trained in mathematics. It is no small merit to have developed a precise conceptualization of German philosophical language!

It was precisely this claim, however, that brought the school-philosophical form and the spelled out systematics into his texts, which later became the subject of clear criticism. This school-philosophical form, which became the form of his philosophy through the mathematical-demonstrative method of developing and deriving each concept from the other, admittedly took up and processed many of Leibniz's thoughts. In its spelled out system form, however, it missed Leibniz's thinking gesture of taking up the systematic thought in many fragments from the problems and rethinking it anew. Kant's expression of the

"Leibniz-Wolff's school philosophy" identifies here two completely different styles of thinking and ignores the fact that Wolff's logical will to order distorts or at least does not properly bring out the speculative dimension of Leibniz's philosophy.

Although Leibniz had recommended Wolff for the mathematics professorship at Halle in 1706, he expressed himself in a letter to Remond not only appreciatively but also reluctantly: "Mr. Wolff has dealt with some of my opinions, but since he is very busy teaching, especially mathematics, and since we have not had much in the way of a common exchange of ideas on philosophy, he can know of my opinions almost only what I have published of them. [...] If he has written something about the soul, in German or otherwise, I will try to meet him to talk about it" (W V, 329 f.). Here, a fundamental difference of philosophical characters is articulated: Wolff sits in school, teaching and reading, while Leibniz is a "networker" and communicator who prefers to discuss things rather than spell them out.

One can show this peculiar unity of closeness of content and distance of thought very well in two of Christian Wolff's writings. In the *Discursus praeliminaris* of his Latin logic, there is a division of philosophy into ontology, *cosmologia generalis*, *psychologia rationalis* and *theologia naturalis*, which exactly in this division will still be the subject of Kant's criticism of metaphysics, in that he proves the impossibility of psychological, cosmological and theological ideas and thus first of all meets Wolff and not Leibniz with it. In his writing *Philosophia Prima Sive Ontologia,* Wolff develops a clearly Leibnizian doctrine of principles. The principle of contradiction and sufficient reason are laid down in Paragraphs 31 and 32 of the *Monadology* as principles of every consideration of reason. Wolff then declines them in his ontology and states that these principles form the basis for the constructive unfolding of the system: "Whoever becomes familiar with our results will therefore be able to progress without difficulty as soon as he has understood the laws of the scientific method and has learned to apply them to practice. The following philosophical works will, however, clearly testify to the fruitfulness of the ontological principles, since what is to be proved there is attributed to them" (Wolff 2005, p. 17).

If we then add to this what this method demands of Wolff, we have in our hands the key to the process of transformation of philosophy that is taking place between Leibniz and Wolff: for this method "demands that every single thing be taught in the place where it can be seen and proven from the preceding" (Wolff 2005, p. 11). At this point, it becomes clear why one cannot speak of a Leibniz-Wolff school philosophy without levelling the difference between Leibniz and Wolff: Wolff takes up the basic principles in order to establish a metaphysics of the understanding and then does something quite different with Leibniz's speculative metaphysics. Leibniz, who presented his systematic basic ideas in a few short metaphysical treatises and otherwise struggled further to specify these basic ideas in a wealth of memoirs and notes, has little in common with this system, which was then indeed presented in a school-like manner.

At one point, however, Wolff shows himself to be a Leibniz pupil who is bolder than his teacher. Leibniz never provoked conflicts and escalation of a political situation—as we have seen, he was thoroughly concerned with reconciliation and compensation. His work on Chinese culture was also influenced by this spirit, which in this case was aimed at cultural exchange. Wolff, on the other hand, did indeed take an interest in the *Sinica* (they were to become fashionable in the chinoiseries of the century anyway), but he did so in such a confrontational manner that after his vice-rectorate speech on the practical philosophy of the Chinese, he was asked to leave Halle and Prussia within 48 h on pain of the rope. He had attacked the Pietists, who were in charge in Halle, and their sanctimonious concept of God. The provocation and the explosive of this speech were to see Confucianism as a rational doctrine that can establish the principles of ethics without reference to a God.

This was not only written in the spirit of Leibniz's faith in reason, but also radicalized it and had to provoke corresponding reactions in Protestant Orthodoxy, which accused Wolff of atheism. Again, the gestures of Leibniz and Wolff could not be more different: Leibniz the irenic, Wolff the rebellious Enlightenment philosopher, who is not deterred even by the gallows from saying clearly what he thinks. In the foreword of 1726, when the speech of 1721 and the expulsion took place some years ago and Wolff has long since been teaching in the safe Marburg, he not only speaks of "certain Leibnizian theses that are inserted into my metaphysical system" (Wolff 1985, p. 9), but also in plain language. The "Chronology of the Chinese" contradicted the creation chronology of the Bible, that is that culture was simply older than the dating of the creation, so that the atheism reproach to lovers of the Chinese culture became even stronger. That did not stop Wolff from defending himself:

> If there is anyone who does not like my work, I ask them to do it better. But if someone is too obtuse to understand the truth, I will reject their judgment as rash. For the following is not written for foolish talkers, nor for the *bigwigs* who are unfamiliar with the sincerity of a Confucius I advise. (Wolff 1985, p. 11)

This is the lively, the upright Wolff, completely without any school-philosophical paragraphs, whom we must always honour in his importance for German culture.

Baumgarten transforms Leibniz in a completely different way. He does not aim at the breadth of a well-formulated system, but at the systematic intensification of some aspects of Leibniz's thinking. Baumgarten uses Leibniz to establish aesthetics as a philosophical discipline. For this appropriation, the concept of the *analogon rationis* is significant because it expresses a similarity between the sensually pre-rational and the structures of reason. Important for the foundation of a philosophical theory of the aesthetic becomes Leibniz' distinction between the truths of reason and the factual truths and his theory of the unconscious. In school philosophy, both theoretical contexts had led to the distinction between upper and lower cognitive faculties. The upper refers to a priori cognitive structures, the lower to cognitions of sensory experience. Baumgarten understands this distinction as an invitation to no longer denounce the realm of sensual experience as a mere source of deception, as happened with Descartes, but to clarify its specific cognitive character.

Sensuality is made presentable, so to speak, with the means of Leibniz metaphysics as a legitimate object of philosophical investigation. Baumgarten makes this clear right at the beginning of his *Aesthetica*, which was published between 1750 and 1758: Possible objections, "sensual sensations, imaginations, fictions—all the confusion of feelings and passions are unworthy of a philosopher," he counters:

> The philosopher is a man among other men, and it is not good if he believes that such an important part of human knowledge is not compatible with his dignity. Confusion is the mother of error. [...] But it is an indispensable condition for the discovery of truth, since nature does not make a leap from darkness into clarity of thought. From the night the way leads only through the dawn to noon. It is precisely for this reason that we must strive for confused knowledge, so that errors do not arise. (Baumgarten 1988, p. 5)

Ex nocte per auroram meridies—that is Leibniz. Baumgarten tries to justify the dignity of sensuality with his theory of the unconscious or the theory of gradual consciousness. Through the *Nouveaux Essais*, it has become known as the theory of *petites perceptions*. However, this work by Leibniz was only published after the appearance of Baumgarten's aesthetics. Leibniz's basic idea is not to limit consciousness to clear and distinct contents, as Descartes did, but to understand it as a clear and distinct section of an infinite number of small, that is semi-conscious or unconscious perceptions below the threshold of clear consciousness, actively produced by the mind itself through directed attention. Leibniz is in this respect the father of the unconscious, though not in the psychological sense as in Freud, but by speaking for the first time of degrees of consciousness intensity.

Baumgarten was able to derive the basic idea from *Monadology*, where Leibniz developed it using the example of stupefaction: "And since one, when awakened from stupefaction, *becomes aware of* one's perceptions, one must therefore have had perceptions immediately before, although one did not become aware of them; for in a natural way a perception can only come from another perception, just as a movement can only come naturally from another movement" (W I, 449). And the following sentence sounds like an invitation to justify aesthetics: "If we did not have something different in our perceptions and, so to speak, something distinguished by a kind of higher taste, we would, as one can see from this, always be in the state of numbness".

With Leibniz's monadological model, Baumgarten fundamentally establishes aesthetics as a perspectival perception of the world. And in the concept of art he takes up Leibniz' concept of possible worlds: He defines it as *veritas heterocosmica*, as the truth of other (possible) worlds (Baumgarten 1988, p. 70). Baumgarten takes up, so to speak, the idea that the real world has excluded other possible worlds by making this world, and not another world, a reality. Art consequently brings other possible worlds, that is alternatives into sensual experience. This is a very modern idea, presented in a somewhat cumbersome, almost scholastic Latin language. As a science of sensual knowledge, aesthetics as a whole becomes a supplement to the logic of understanding: clarity and distinctness mean, as Leibniz showed, an abstraction from the complexity of confused sensual experience. Aesthetics in Baumgarten's sense is intended to organize this experience by arranging the sensually chaotic appearing manifold into a unity. In this sense, Leibniz' philosophy has become the impetus for a new science.

Changed Reception Conditions: Lessing and Herder

In the 1760s, the reception situation changed fundamentally. Anyone who holds in their hands the edition of the *Opera Omnia* published in Geneva in 1768 is met by the aura of the century: The beautiful, strong leather binding, the rough but still intact paper after 250 years, the leaflet with the portrait engraving in the first volume, which also contains the *Leibnitii Vita* of Jacob Brucker, from whom the eighteenth century drew its philosophical and historical knowledge about Leibniz—all this radiates appreciation for the great universal scholar. The edition brings together the then well-known Leibniz: writings on theology, in the second volume logic and metaphysics, but also physics, medicine, botany and natural history, then mathematical writings, philosophy, history and jurisprudence, even philological writings. The whole diversity of a Leibniz scattered until then in the overview of one edition—that was the great achievement of Dutens.

Already in 1765, there had been the edition of *Oeuvres philosophiques* published by Raspe in Amsterdam and Leipzig, which for the first time contained the *Nouveaux Essais*, that critical examination of John Locke, which Leibniz had not published out of reverence because Locke had just died. Now, in the coming Sturm und Drang, the work will encounter greatly altered conditions of reception. In addition, an examination of Spinoza gradually began in Germany, which will strongly influence the Leibniz image from Lessing (1995a) to Goethe (1981c).

But what did the self-confident enlightener Lessing do in 1773 in the face of so many newly edited works by Leibniz? He made a find in the Wolfenbüttel library, for which the court librarian Leibniz himself had once been responsible, and presented it to the interested public. To make a long story short: Leibniz had wanted to publish a work by Ernst Soner, a delicate undertaking, because Soner represented the heterodox theses of the Sozinians, a religious movement that denied central dogmas of the Church such as the divinity of Christ, the Trinity, original sin and the eternity of hell punishments. Leibniz had already written a preface to this, but then apparently abandoned the delicate project. The preface remained in Wolfenbüttel, the successor in office, the librarian Lessing, finds it and makes it public in his text under the title "Leibniz of the eternal punishments".

Let us summarize the highly interesting argumentation: Leibniz, according to Lessing, says in this preface that hell-punishments, if they exist (which Leibniz does not comment on) must necessarily be eternal. In a most interesting way, Lessing takes up the distinction between exoteric and acroamatic speech, which we know from the context of the theodicy problem: With his statement about eternal punishment Leibniz did "nothing more and nothing less than what all old philosophers used to do in their *exoteric* discourse. He observed a wisdom for which, of course, our newest philosophers have become much too wise. He willingly set his system aside; and sought to lead everyone on the path to truth on which he found it" (Lessing 1995b, p. 89).

And what will become acroamatic, that is in metaphysical severity, then at all from the hell-punishments? According to Leibniz Lessing, "nothing can be determined about it" (Lessing 1995b, p. 91). If one accepts the precondition of hell-punishments, Lessing continues, then they must be eternal, because according to Leibniz's system everything we do has infinite consequences. Lessing thus states a philosophical rationalization of theological questions in the spirit of *Theodicy*. In the end, only the *eternity* of hell-punishments can be rationally justified, but not the question whether such hell-punishments exist at all. The hermeneutic conclusion to abolish them as mere metaphorics of the Bible is then taken over by the disputatious Enlightenment philosopher Lessing himself: "For by taking almost all images from the physical pain, Scripture, in order to arouse the most vivid imagination of that unhappiness that waits for the wicked" (Lessing 1995b, p. 98), but by misunderstanding the metaphorical character of this speech, the idea of hell came about. If this metaphorical character is understood and if, with Leibniz, the only exoteric—to put it bluntly: the pedagogical—meaning of the speech is grasped by eternal hell punishments, then the reality of hell becomes invalid. So the "famous Mr Leibniz" helps to abolish hell.

Herder's *Journal of my journey in 1769* had heralded the sensitivity of Sturm und Drang. Thus the theory of the smallest perceptions, of *petites perceptions*, as it was called in the recently published *Nouveaux Essais*, was placed in a context that was completely alien to the original rationalist concern to rationally determine the pre-rational (Baumgarten had shown in a field such as aesthetics how a rationalist continuation of Leibniz's theses was possible), but nevertheless claimed the theory. In 1774, in his book *Vom Erkennen und Empfinden der menschlichen Seele (i.e., On the Recognition and Sensation of the Human Soul)*, Herder attempted to explain why recognition and perception cannot be separated. Up to this point this would still correspond to Leibniz's intentions. The essential unity of body and soul, which Herder represents, can also refer to the metaphysics of Leibniz, who himself as an Aristotelian had argued against the Cartesian separation.

The problem begins at the point where Herder positions sensibility against the rationalist philosophy of the Enlightenment: "It is against such abysses of dark sentiments, forces, and stimuli that our bright and clear philosophy is most terrified of. It blesses itself against it as the hell of lowest soul forces and prefers to play on the Leibniz chessboard with some deaf words and classifications of dark and clear, distinct and confused ideas [...]" (Herder 1969, p. 17f.). This clearly refers to Wolff or also Baumgarten, and accuses them of having rationalized away the dark sensations—which, as we have seen, is simply not true. What is clearly noticeable, however, is the intention, which cannot be reconciled with Leibniz at all, to romanticize the unity of body and soul or of cognition and feeling. This attempt is clearly noticeable in the choice of language:

> In nature, nothing is divorced at all, everything flows through imperceptible transitions to and into each other [...] Nobody said it better than Leibniz that the body as such is only a phenomenon of substances, like the Milky Way of stars and the cloud of drops. Leibniz even tried to explain motion as an appearance of an inner state which we do not know, but which could be a representation, because we do

not know any inner state. ... All the passions, stored around the heart and stimulating all sorts of tools, hang together by invisible bonds and take root in the finest structure of our soulful fibres. (Herder 1969, p. 16)

Here, we see a linguistic transition to an irrationalistic view of Leibniz: everything flows (indistinguishably) into one another, movement becomes an expression of inwardness, just as the whole gesture of language is "stored around the heart" and thus makes things unrecognisable. But this is reliably not Leibniz: for he considered the undistinguished and confused to be unrecognised, but not unrecognisable. The *petites perceptions* then become definitively protoromantic a few pages further on: the thinking of the human soul "will only come out of sentiment; its servants and angels, messengers of air and flames will pour out their food to it, just as these only live in its will. It rules to speak with Leibniz, in a realm of slumbering but all the more intimately dormant beings" (Herder 1969, p. 30).

This is really a good example of the inherent dynamics of reception processes in the history of ideas: the original intention of Leibniz's theory of consciousness, to make the undistinguishable, the confused clear, and to widen our concept of consciousness, is turned into its opposite, namely more indistinguishable, more confused—and through the enhancement of sensitivity the field of possible consciousness is even made narrower. If Leibniz's writing had appeared immediately after it was written, it would have had quite different conditions of reception at the beginning of the century and would not have been so easily stimulated to fish in the mud. *Habent sua fata libelli*—books also have their fate because their delayed publication means that they are sometimes perceived in a perspective that does not do them justice.

"Deceptive Terms." Kant and the Consequences

Kant occupied himself with Leibniz throughout his life. His first work, *Gedanken von der wahren Schätzung der lebendigen Kräfte* (*Thoughts on the True Estimation of the Living Forces*), written between 1746 and 1749, is Kant's attempt "to act as an arbitrator between Cartesians and Leibnizians in the dispute over how to measure the magnitude of the moving force" (Gulyga 1985, p. 24). Already the pre-critical Kant is a unifier of school directions, just as later the critical Kant will try to unite rationalism and empiricism in transcendental philosophy: "In this writing he tries to unite Descartes and Leibniz, at a mature age he does so with the main philosophical schools" (Gulyga 1985, p. 26). But there is an essential difference: the pre-critical Kant deals objectively with concrete problems of Leibniz's philosophy, while Leibniz in his critical work gets into the mills of the fundamental metaphysical criticism of the "Alleszermalmer".

In his *Attempt at some reflections on optimism* from 1759 (in the same year the *Candide* was published) Kant gives a more appropriate account of Leibniz than Voltaire had done: "This world is the best of all possible worlds", it "is the best that could have been produced"; he also sees with sympathy that Leibniz is working against an arbitrary god who simply says: "I liked it, and that is enough" (Kant 1983a, p. 587). According to his own statement, Kant is still in the "dogmatic slumber" of his lively master's years, when he is almost a little authoritarian with Leibniz. If "one is in agreement with me: that among all possible worlds one is necessarily the most perfect, then I demand not to argue further. [...] One makes very poor use of philosophy when one uses it to reverse the principles of common sense reason" (Kant 1983a, p. 592). Common sense demands the basic idea of theodicy, and Kant takes a very pre-critical view of this point.

And he goes one better when he lets Leibniz almost anticipate the critique of reason. There are "as Leibniz remarks deceptive terms (notiones deceptrices), of which it seems that one thinks something through them, but which in fact do not represent anything" (Kant 1983a, p. 590). This is exactly what the Kant of transcendental philosophy will later accuse metaphysics in general and of course then also Leibniz. For the moment, he wants to "learn to see" what he will later categorically exclude as knowledge: *that the whole is the best,* and *everything is good for the sake of the whole*" (Kant 1983a, p. 594).

After his awakening from the "dogmatic slumber" he will write *about the failure of all philosophical attempts in theodicy* and "advocate the cause of God" and then call it the cause of a "presumptuous reason that misjudges its limits" (Kant 1983b, p. 105). A justification of God requires "omniscience", which is impossible in the experiential world of phenomena. Here, Kant argues completely on the metaphysical-critical line of his Critical Philosophy, which prohibits a possible experience-transcending use of the concepts of reason—and thus also the theodicy: "that our reason is simply incapable of understanding *the relationship in which a world, as we may always know it through experience, stands to the highest wisdom*" (Kant 1983b, p. 114). In other words, whether God had to choose this world and could not choose any other, we cannot know about it—for the same reason, however, also the critical "objections" of the opponents of theodicy must fail, because they too "cannot prove the contrary" (Kant 1983b). So it is better not to talk about it at all. Philosophy enters an age in which it will have to keep silent about many things.

Exactly on the threshold from pre-critical Kant to his transcendental turn, the philosopher from Königsberg tackled a problem on which Leibniz had contradicted Newton. Leibniz had discussed this question of the relativity of space in his correspondence with Samuel Clarke, published in 1717 and therefore known to the interested public. In the 1768 paper, *Von dem ersten Grund des Unterschiedenes der Gegenden im Raume (Of the first reason for the difference of regions in space),* Kant, with all due respect, already distanced himself: "The famous *Leibniz* possessed many real insights, through which he enriched the sciences, but even much greater designs for those whose execution the world expected of him in vain" (Kant 1983c, p. 993). Kant says nothing less here than that Leibniz failed to prove his thesis of the relativity of space, which he held against Newton.

Let's take a quick look at what Leibniz said in the letters to Clarke:

> These gentlemen consider that *space* is a real absolute being; but this leads to great difficulties. For it seems as if this being must be eternal and infinite. [...] As far as I am concerned, I have emphasized more than once that I consider *space* as well as *time* to be something purely relative, for an order of coexistence of existences, just as time is an order of their succession. Because space, if you look at it in its mere possibility, is an order of things that exist at the same time and as far as they are together, without saying anything about their special way of existing. And when one sees several things together, one becomes aware of this order of things. (WV, 371f.)

Leibniz understands space as *ordre des coexistences,* that is in the sense of his metaphysics of compossibility as an order of individual things that relate to each other; it is relative because it represents a structural order that is constituted by the relationship of things. Kant, on the other hand, argues for the homogeneous and absolute space of modern physics, that is, Newton: later, in the *Critique of Pure Reason*, he will speak of space as a transcendental condition a priori and distinguish between the empirical reality of space as a space of experience and the transcendental ideality of space as a condition of the possibility of experience. This is also already his argument in the essay of 1768: the actual experience of incongruent counterparts such as the right and the left hand and of incongruent spaces in general does not show for Kant precisely the relativity of space, but rather the objective independence of space as a condition of such phenomena of experience. In a word, the famous Leibniz had not understood that space is not an object but a condition of perception, and Kant did not owe the "counter-evidence".

To summarize the position that the classical Kant of the *Critique of Pure Reason* takes on metaphysics, it makes sense to use the *Prolegomena*, because in this writing, which summarizes the results of his metaphysical criticism from his major work, Kant explicitly poses the question of the possibility of a future metaphysics. He turns the criticism of the metaphysical way of thinking into the positive question of how metaphysics could be possible as a science. In the whole structure of the argumentation—criticism of the psychological idea of the immortality of the soul, the cosmological question of finiteness or infinity of the world, the theological idea as a philosophical question of the existence of God—Kant's orientation towards the structure of Christian Wolff's school metaphysics is evident. That Leibniz is nevertheless affected by the criticism becomes clear when one considers Kant's main argument, which underlies all refutations. Reason is to be limited to a use that constitutes experience and every metaphysics that makes use of the concepts of reason beyond experience is to be made inadmissible. The monad, however, is not an object of possible experience, but rather a transempirical model concept for the structure of the world whole that can never be given in experience.

Kant argues in a very summarised way as follows: metaphysics deduces from the substance character of the soul its persistence or imperishability. If one now starts from what is accessible to experience, one cannot draw this latter conclusion: "Now the subjective condition of all our possible experience is life: consequently, one can only conclude on the persistence of the soul in life, for the death of man is the end of all experience. [...] Therefore, the soul's perseverance can only be shown in the life of man (the proof of which we will probably be given) but not after death (which is what we really want)" (Kant 1983d, p. 206 f.). The immortality of the soul is transcendent in experience and thus the question about it is illegitimate within the limits of the critique of reason.

And so Kant also rejects cosmological speculations: If one bases the criterion of the verifiability of metaphysical statements on experience, one must simply abstain from a judgement when it is about the decision whether the world is eternal or has a beginning. And also in the ontological proof of God this tendency of reason to go beyond the scope of experience is effective. It is only logical determinations and not something verifiable in experience that derives the existence of God from the concept of his perfection (which must then include existence), thus out of the hat as the magician conjures the rabbit.

After the end of his critical business, in 1791 Kant made one last statement on metaphysics and also on Leibniz, namely in his answer to the prize question that had been put on hold by, of all places, the Academy of Sciences in Berlin, which Leibniz had founded: *What are the real advances that metaphysics has made in Germany since Leibniz and Wolff's time?* Kant's answer is (how could it be otherwise?) that these advances have occurred in transcendental philosophy: The text is a nice summary of the main theses of Kant's critique of reason, and then also comes to speak of the "fallacy of attempts to concede objective reality to the concepts of understanding, even without sensuality" (Kant 1983e, p. 614), in order to cash in on Leibniz's entire doctrine of principles by pointing out the lack of a unity of concept and perception: Whether these attempts in metaphysics ascribed to Leibniz and Wolff "deserve to be called progress in metaphysics" must "be left to the judgement of those who are not misled by great names" (Kant 1983e, p. 620). The "famous Leibniz" has come to its end under the verdict of the critique of reason. We know today that this was not the case.

"Strike Fire from Every Pebble": Was Goethe a Leibnizian?

This question is usually answered negatively in research. What is certain is that the Leibniz picture of the classical epoch of German culture was shaped by the debate about Spinoza, which Friedrich Heinrich Jacobi triggered in 1785 with his Spinoza book. In it, Jacobi describes his conversation with Lessing, in which he is said to have confessed to being a Spinoza scholar. In the account of this conversation, however, Lessing also merged Spinoza and Leibniz: "I fear that [Leibniz, J.Z.] was himself a Spinozist at heart. *I:* Are you talking seriously? *Lessing: Do* you seriously doubt it?" Then Lessing talks about his respect for Leibniz, and Jacobi says the famous words: "Quite right. Leibniz liked to make fire out of every pebble." (Jacobi 2000, p. 29). Jacobi—and not Lessing!—has pretty much established the topos that Leibniz can be understood from Spinoza. In addition, with Jacobi's book and the delicate question of a commitment to pantheism (which in those days meant as much as the accusation of atheism), the question of Spinoza was simply more burning on the nails. It is not about interpreting Goethe as a Leibnizian, but simply to show that there are motives in Goethe that can be understood much better with Leibniz than with Spinoza.

In the text *Einwirkung der neueren Philosophie* the name "Leibniz" does not appear. However, Goethe reports that he read Jacob Brucker's history of philosophy as a child. So he must have heard of Leibniz. Goethe did not find any connection to philosophy in general: "I had no organ for philosophy in the true sense of the word" (Goethe 1981d, p. 25). Goethe then reports that Kant's *Critique of pure reason* was "completely outside my circle" (Goethe 1981d, p. 26) and only the *Critique of judgement* with its unity of aesthetics and teleology of nature brought Kant close to him. And precisely here lies the reason for his approach to Spinoza: it is the conception of nature as a whole, not logic and metaphysics, that leads him on his excursions into philosophy.

So in the *Study according to Spinoza*: "But the infinite or the complete existence cannot be thought by us. We can only think things that are either limited, or that our soul is limiting for us. So we have a concept of the infinite in so far as we can think that there is a complete existence, which is beyond the comprehension of a limited mind. We cannot say that the infinite has parts" (Goethe 1981c, p. 7). This is Spinoza: the one substance of nature whose attributes are the limited mind and finite things (that is, what dualistically fell apart at Descartes as *res cogitans* and *res extensa*). And Goethe says something else interesting: we cannot have a finite concept of infinity, but we can have a *concept* of infinity. That would be precisely the argument of metaphysics against Kant's critique of reason.

Then it becomes highly interesting to ask about the motives of Leibniz's thinking: for Goethe speaks of "the souls that have an inner strength" and of "that all living things have their relationship within themselves" (Goethe 1981c, pp. 8 and 9). This is *not* to be thought of in this way with Spinoza, but rather in a Leibnizian way: the step from the mechanical (which Spinoza's nature alone has in mind) to the living organic of nature is still conceivable from Kant's *Critique of judgement*; "inner strength" and "having the relationship in oneself", on the other hand, are basic ideas of Leibniz. It is therefore significant that Goethe, precisely at the systematic point where he is not concerned with the mechanical connection of nature, but with the living totality of the organic whole of nature, falls back on these motifs of Leibniz's thinking.

In the so-called *Urphänomen*, the central concept of Goethe's philosophy of nature, the whole of nature presents itself as a limited object of contemplation. In this limited appearance, the whole is revealed; consequently, Goethe is not concerned with the isolated singularity of a phenomenon in Kant's sense, but with a general appearance that appears in the individual. The relationship between the individual natural phenomenon and the whole of nature is conceived by Goethe in the form of a universal analogy relationship. He clearly expressed this in an aphorism of *Maxims and reflections*: "Every existing thing is an analog of everything existing; therefore, existence always appears to us at the same time separate and connected. If one follows the analogy too closely, everything collapses identically; if one avoids it, everything scatters into infinity" (Goethe 1981b, p. 368).

The context of the whole is thus also here conceived as a unity of relationships, and in this unity each individual is then somehow similar to all the others—just as Leibniz had said about the monads. In the fragment quoted, Goethe also attempts to grasp independent being for oneself and being related to others as moments of phenomena. Thinking in analogies seeks the middle, which neither fixes identity in an egalitarian way nor dissolves everything into disparate multiplicity. This is exactly what Goethe tries to achieve in his philosophical thinking about nature. The name Leibniz does not come up, and yet the monad model seems to be the most suitable way to substantiate Goethe's intuition that every single existing thing is an analogue of everything existing in an overall philosophical concept.

Leibniz is even in the *Faust*. Unnamed and in this case not so clearly visible, but nevertheless justifiable: The Faustian motif of unfinished striving, which is the subject of the famous wager (Mephistopheles gets Faust's soul if the latter is ever satisfied with what he has achieved and says to the moment: "Stay but, you are so beautiful"), can be compared with Leibniz's concept of happiness with profit. The basic motif of *Faust* even finds its exact philosophical equivalent in Leibniz: "Happiness does not consist in a supreme degree, but in a constant growth of joys" (W I, 373). Here, Leibniz articulates a profoundly modern conception of man and understanding of happiness, which is symbolically represented in the Faust drama. In the *Nouveaux Essais* there is a sentence that reads like a commentary on the Faust Bet: "*Far from considering this restlessness incompatible with happiness,* I find that restlessness is essential for creatures' happiness, which never consists in a perfect possession that would make them insensitive and, as it were, dull, but in a constant and uninterrupted progress towards the greatest goods, which must be accompanied by a desire or at least by a constant restlessness" (W I, 373; W III.1, 291 f.). This is precisely the theme and leitmotif of the "Faust" drama.

Leibniz in German Idealism: Schelling and Hegel

Schelling also moves Leibniz closer to Spinoza. In the development of German idealism between Fichte's philosophy of the ego and Hegel's philosophy of mind, he himself had argued in terms of natural philosophy and even published a *Journal for Speculative Physics*. His early main work from 1800, the *System of Transcendental Idealism,* attempted to establish the identity of nature and spirit. Spinoza's pantheism played a not insignificant role in this. This connection is also retained in the lectures on the history of modern philosophy held much later, namely in 1833/1834 in Munich, in which Leibniz is also mentioned, although the revolutionary days of German Idealism in the Biedermeier era are over and after Hegel and Goethe's death a period of conservative paralysis begins. Schelling, however, "even in the Munich lectures he still expresses his inclination towards Spinozism, which fertilized the pantheism of young Schelling" (Holz 2015, p. 76).

Now Schelling, as far as Leibniz's approach to Spinoza is concerned, is entirely in the tradition of Jacobi. But as so often in the course of reception, the thesis, in which Schelling remains quite true to himself, gets a different flavour in changed time courses: for the approach to Spinoza now means that Schelling understands Leibniz' concept of God in the sense that it is "a supreme concept of the world", that is to say: "Leibniz was considered to be an atheist to him, which Spinoza already was" (Holz 2015, p. 70). In a post-revolutionary time, the same ideas are then no longer taken up affirmatively, but provided with critical distance. First Schelling reports that Leibniz was wrongly seen as being in tacit opposition to Spinoza, only to then open up the series of his agreements with him. Schelling correctly sees the position against Descartes in the body-mind problem: "Leibniz was a resolute anti-dualist, the physical and the spiritual were one in so far as he attributed both to the concept of monas" (von Schelling 1985, p. 468f.). But then he emphasizes the similarity with Spinoza in this question, which implicitly immediately brings the problem to a head with the question of atheism: for whoever represents the unity of body and soul denies the immortality of the soul (which Leibniz reliably had not done so and Schelling even only hints at). Spinoza is then in this respect the more consistent thinker, and Schelling can regard "Leibnizianism at first only as a stunted Spinozism" (von Schelling 1985, p. 470).

In the conservative context of the Munich lectures and the epoch after the Congress of Vienna, such statements, which could also be positively received (and in Spinoza's case in better days had been positively received by Schelling), get a discrediting, suspicious undertone, which in times of the night watchman state does not even have to be spoken out openly. Leibniz as one of the outstanding representatives of enlightened spirit in Germany is suspected of having been an atheist like Spinoza.

The inclusion of the romanticizing topos of the sleeping monads, which we already know from Herder, is then correspondingly logical:

> we must praise at least one meritorious side of him, that is, that he was not content to speak of things only *in abstracto*,

without regard to their differences and gradations. *Leibniz* first called the world of inorganic bodies, which were generally called dead, a *sleeping* monad world; the soul of plants and animals was to him the merely *dreaming* monas, the rational soul the waking one. Although he expressed this gradation only metaphorically, it should not be overlooked. It was the first beginning to look at the One Being of Nature in the necessary sequence of stages of its coming to itself, and in this respect can be regarded as the first germ of later, more lively development. This page is still the most beautiful and best of the Leibniz teaching. (von Schelling 1985, p. 470)

Here, the dialectic of the course of reception becomes very clear, but also the subtlety of the shifts in meaning that take place. Schelling argues as the philosopher of identity philosophy and its unity of nature and spirit that he has been. He claims Leibniz as the forerunner for this, saying that he has taken up the metaphors existing at Leibniz and does it better. The whole thing, however, happens in a way that itself alludes to the night metaphor of the romantic "moon world" of sleep-dreaming. Irrationalizations of a rationalist: "Certainly Leibniz's spirit is further along than he has let on. He was gifted, as it were, with a magical gaze, a gaze to which every object to which he attached himself unlocked itself as if by itself" (von Schelling 1985, p. 475). The "most beautiful" of Leibniz's teaching is thus actually identical with the "best" of Schelling's teaching.

Another aspect makes Schelling's portrayal highly interesting: the discovery of Leibniz as a historical figure. The eighteenth century dealt with Leibniz's arguments in an almost contemporary way, had no historical distance to him and did not yet reflect on his historical position and function. Schelling, however, is aware of this historical significance in the historically conscious nineteenth century: "If he did not achieve all that he could with such great qualities, one must consider the insurmountable death of his time, that sad time in Germany that immediately followed the disruptions of the Thirty Years' War". Through this historical achievement, he will "always remain a pride of the German nation"; and it is "his spirit, more mediating than revolutionary," which enables him to become this model of the cultural nation (von Schelling 1985). That is correctly presented and yet somehow wrong. In the upheavals and divisions of German history, language and culture are the continuous element that also creates unity. It becomes wrong in context and its connotations: Schelling speaks of Leibniz as a "mediator", not in a post-war period under the precept of peace, but in a post-revolutionary, restorative period of an awakening nationalism, which certainly did not correspond to Leibniz's intentions, but which are now to be instrumentalised for it.

Perspectives open up certain insights, but they always mean blinkers. Hegel sees Leibniz correctly in many respects, for example his "bustle", which has "roamed" around in various sciences (Hegel 1971, pp. 234 and 236). He is close to the dialectical Leibniz—and yet he is not willing to access it. Thus he contradicts the view, widespread in his time, that Leibniz was understood from Spinoza: "Leibniz [...] contrasts Spinoza with the infinite multiplicity of individuals" (Hegel 1971, p. 197). In the *Encyclopedia*, he called metaphysics "the *unbiased* method", which "contains the *belief that* through *reflection* the *truth is recognized*, that what the objects truly are is brought before consciousness" (Hegel 1970, p. 93). This proved Kant right against the "former" metaphysics, where he was right, that is in the criticism of the naivety of the standpoint of all metaphysics of understanding, which in it equals a philosophically unreflected procedure: "All initial philosophy, all sciences, yes, even the daily doing and driving of consciousness lives in this belief" (Hegel 1970).

But Hegel's real question to Leibniz is how he thinks the infinite whole. And first of all he emphasizes that this is precisely what he is concerned with: Leibniz "claimed that thinking is opposed to English perception [...] Spinoza is the general, *a* substance. With Locke, we saw the finite determinations as the basis. The basic principle of Leibniz is the individual" (Hegel 1971, p. 233). It is therefore a matter of making this individual the principle of the foundation of the whole. And here, Hegel accuses Leibniz of not being systematic enough in this matter: his philosophy is less a "philosophical system" than it is "a hypothesis". These are "thoughts, which, by the way, are presented in a narrative fashion without any consequence of the concept as a whole". Leibniz' philosophy is then merely "a metaphysical novel" (Hegel 1971, p. 238). Exactly that allows us to be so close to Leibniz today, the hypothetical and also fragmentary lecture, precisely the openness of his thoughts, becomes a shortcoming for the closed systematist Hegel: "His philosophy is therefore scattered all over in small brochures, letters, answers to objections; we find no elaborated systematic whole. The work that looks something like this, his *Théodicée,* the most famous among the public, is a popular writing" and "no longer quite enjoyable for us" (Hegel 1971, p. 236). Hegel thus brings his own, systematically closed concept of philosophy to Leibniz.

His philosophical-historical account mentions all the essential elements of Leibniz's thought that could have led Hegel to a dialectical understanding: first of all "the very important determination" that "in the substance itself" "negativity" is contained (Hegel 1971, p. 242). In Hegel's language, this means: the individual substance has the relationship to the other in itself. He further speaks of the "spontaneity of the monad" and that change is based on its activity (Hegel 1971, p. 243). He sees very clearly that Leibniz conceives the pre-stabilized harmony as a unity of relationships (all elements of dialectical thinking)—and then complains that he conceives it "as a relationship without concepts" (Hegel 1971, p. 250). At this point, however, an essential difference between Hegel and Leibniz is expressed: Hegel always thinks relationships in the form of the concept, whereas Leibniz' system understands world as a unity of real relationships.

Hegel is even quite aware of the perspectivism we have worked out: "From *a* grain of sand, the whole universe could be understood in its entire development, if we could fully recognize the grain of sand. [...] Thus, every monad has or is the idea of the whole universe, i.e., it is an idea in general, but at the same time a certain one, whereby it is this monad, an idea according to its special situation and circumstances" (Hegel 1971, p. 253). Hegel sees the point of Leibniz's philosophy very precisely—and disguises himself in the name of the concept, that is a closed dialectic of concepts that Leibniz "did not know how to carry out" (Hegel 1971). We would like to assume that he did not want to carry it out in this way.

Perspectives on Leibniz

When Leibniz's house in Hanover was torn down in the middle of the nineteenth century, Ludwig Kugelmann sent some scraps of wallpaper from Leibniz's study that had been found in the overburden, to his friend Karl Marx in London. Marx framed it and hung it up in his own study. The beautiful story has been handed down because Marx told it in a letter to Engels, not without adding: "You know my admiration for Leibniz" (see Holz 2015, p. 55f.). A beautiful picture for reception: framed fragments. An enlightening picture for Marx, who very early made excerpts from Leibniz (Marx 1976, p. 183 ff.). An apt image also for the relationship of the century to tradition: demolitions create a need for storage.

This is exactly what is happening with the Leibniz legacy. For in the post-classical period, as in so many other respects, the spirits of Leibniz's reception were divided. On the one hand, we have Ludwig Feuerbach, who in the nineteenth century was the philosophical-historical successor to Hegel and represented the beginning of the scientific study of

Leibniz's philosophy with his monographic account of Leibniz. Behind this intensive occupation lies, of course, his own philosophical approach, which understands the speculative tradition of philosophy from Spinoza via Leibniz to Hegel as transformed theology or God transformed into reason: "It is therefore an inner, a sacred *necessity* that the essence of reason, which is distinguished from reason, is finally *identified with reason*, that the divine essence is thus recognized, realized and made present *as the essence of reason. The high historical significance* of *speculative philosophy* is based on this necessity" (Feuerbach 1982, p. 266f.). Thus, Feuerbach can then interpret Leibniz as the precursor of his materialism (Feuerbach 1982, p. 275). His merit, however, is a thorough monographic presentation, which is to work out the "high historical significance".

On the other hand, Arthur Schopenhauer can be mentioned as an example, who articulates the lack of understanding of the Leibniz era. He rejects the positive appropriation of Leibniz by the German idealists: they wanted to return "to the muddy channel of old dogmatism […] and entertainingly go on […] talking about their well-known, recommended favorite subjects […] This is where the affectionate veneration and praise of Leibniz, which has been spreading everywhere for several years now, comes from. But now, *held against Kant*, Leibniz is a pitiful little light" (Schopenhauer 1988a, p. 180f.). This degrading language speaks for itself of his fame, which was widespread in his time, and for himself. Schopenhauer can only scold "about Leibniz's system […], high esteem gives proof that the absurd is the easiest to make happiness in the world" (Schopenhauer 1988b, p. 14). This accusation immediately fell back on its author when suddenly "widespread fame" came over the philosopher Schopenhauer, who in Frankfurt at his salon window handed his opera glasses to the soldiers shooting at the barricade fighters for the first German democracy.

The nineteenth century was otherwise unspectacular in its relationship to Leibniz. But in its philological industriousness it was very important for the development in the twentieth century, because only the gradual creation of an appropriate source began to put the "Leibniz" puzzle together. This then enabled various perspectives on his work, because it could be made visible in its many facets through a comprehensive edition. The history of their edition is therefore always of outstanding importance for the reception of classical authors. In the case of Leibniz, this is all the more true because his work is a *puzzle of many small pieces.* In contrast, for example, to the philosophies of the classical period between Kant and Hegel, where there were always systematic main works that perhaps did not reveal all the facets, but did broadly develop the essential idea, there were only a few main writings by Leibniz and one popular work that acted more as a barrier to reception.

The great topicality of Leibniz and his appeal for our thinking today, however, consists precisely in the fact that he constantly rethinks the systematic content of his thinking in the fragmentary form of drafts. Leibniz thinks as if in a workshop—but the thoughts filed on thousands of slips of paper for reconsideration and the exchange of ideas in letters remained closed to Leibniz's understanding and interpretation for a long time. This very situation began to change with the actual history of the edition in the nineteenth century. The edition of the *Philosophische Schriften*—(*Philosophical Writings*) procured by Gerhardt from 1875 to 1890 is still the standard edition for philosophical Leibniz research.

The complete edition of the *Sämtliche Schriften und Briefe* (*Complete Writings and Letters*) has been putting the puzzle together since 1923 and moves the resulting overall picture through the twentieth century, so to speak: the edition was begun during the Weimar Republic by the Prussian Academy of Sciences, continued in the GDR as an Academy edition and after 1990 was continued by the Berlin-Brandenburg and Göttingen Academies of Sciences and Humanities. The Leibniz Archives in Hanover, the Leibniz Research Centre in Münster and the Leibniz Research Centre in Berlin are involved in the edition. This is a large undertaking that is far from being completed. This is why the bilingual student edition of the *Philosophical Writings*, which has been published by the Wissenschaftliche Buchgesellschaft in Darmstadt since 1959, is very useful for general study use: among other things, because under the reception conditions of the twenty-first century, it can no longer be assumed without further ado that a generally interested reader will read Latin and French.

It is impossible to give an overview of the intensive and wide-ranging Leibniz research in this short presentation, which is based on the important editions. In his introduction to such an overview of research, Albert Heinekamp writes very aptly: "One creates Leibniz anew without ceasing" (Heinekamp /Schupp 1988, p. 3). However, the twentieth century brought a significant new development in the Leibniz image with the discovery of the logician Leibniz by Bertrand Russell and Louis Couturat. *Systematic* perspectives on Leibniz developed: Ernst Cassirer discovered the philosopher of consciousness Leibniz and Hans Heinz Holz the dialectician.

It seems as if the reception in the twentieth century wanted to confirm the perspectivism that Leibniz himself had philosophically founded. Among other things, this states that—provided there is hermeneutic rigour—no position can be completely wrong, but neither can any position have the exclusive right on its side. Perspectives shed light on aspects and focus on the object of interpretation, but also lose sight of other things. What Leibniz said about metaphysical models probably applies to these interpretative perspectives: they are hypotheses, and the one that can explain more aspects of Leibniz is more convincing. Discussing the correctness or falsity of these perspectives requires an exhaustive discussion, which is not possible in our context. However, one must at least briefly characterize and reconstruct these different perspectives of the twentieth century in order to be able to more precisely grasp the question of "Leibniz today", that is its significance for the future in the twenty-first century.

The Topicality of the Logician Leibniz: Bertrand Russell

In 1945, almost half a century after his groundbreaking study of Leibniz, Russell treated him from the perspective of a philosophy historian, which in turn, however, expressed nothing more than Russell's systematic view of Leibniz. Russell distinguished between a popular exoteric doctrine articulated in the theological and metaphysical work that Leibniz himself intended for publication, and an esoteric doctrine that he had excluded from publication and which now came to light through the new editions: the doctrine of the logician Leibniz. This secret doctrine, of which one does not quite understand why Leibniz should have withheld it, showed the essential point: "Leibniz was firmly convinced of the importance of logic, not only in its own field, but also as the basis of metaphysics. He was working on a mathematical logic that would have become immensely important if he had published it" (Russell 2012, p. 600).

It would have "replaced thinking with calculating". This characterization makes Leibniz the forerunner of mathematical logic as the basis of philosophy in general (for it is not only valid "in its own field" as in traditional philosophy, but as the basis of thinking in general). Russell consistently adheres to this interpretation, seeing metaphysics as founded in logic (and not, which is after all conceivable, letting the form of logic emerge from the metaphysical concept): "The concept of substance [...] is derived from the logical category of subject and predicate" (Russell 2012, p. 599). Russell thus "perspectively" claims Leibniz for his own programmatic approach to a philosophy based on mathematical logic: "In his thinking closed to the public, Leibniz is the best example of a philosopher who uses logic as the key to metaphysics" (Russell 2012, p. 603).

This view stylizes the discovery of the logician Leibniz, which is without doubt a significant achievement. In *A Critical Exposition of the Philosophy of Leibniz* (1900), Russell develops the logician Leibniz from the *Discours de Métaphysique* and the correspondence with Arnauld, which belongs in this context. It has been repeatedly emphasized that Russell discovered Leibniz's contribution to the logic of relational propositions. But it is precisely this really very important problem, whether the relations are external and coincidental to the subject or *belong* essentially *to* him (we have seen how important this question is in Leibniz's metaphysics), that shows how difficult it is to clarify the question of the relationship between logic and metaphysics. Questions arise about the ontological status, that is, about the reality of relations. Do they have a lesser reality compared to the substance? Does the mind add the relations or are they something? In his metaphysical conception, Leibniz had included the relationship in the concept of substance.

So it seems difficult to derive Leibniz's metaphysics from logic without further ado. For metaphysical statements are ontological statements, that is statements about the constitution of reality, whereas logic tests and determines the *formal* character of propositions. As soon as logic is regarded as the fundamental, a uniformity of thinking and being is *presupposed*, although it would first have to be *justified* in order to decide the question. So we leave the question as a question—and thank Russell for *posing* the problem of a logic of relation. Shortly after him, Louis Couturat (1901) also underlined the importance of logic in Leibniz's thinking. He brought less of his own systematic presuppositions than Russell and argues more historically; but Couturat also comes to the conclusion that metaphysics is derived from logic: "The monad is the logical subject elevated to substance; its attributes become the accidentals 'inherent' to the essence of substance" (Couturat 1988, p. 61).

The seminal aspect of Leibniz's contribution to logic is indeed, as Russell emphasized, the attempt to *formalize* it or to make it a system of symbolic signs. The *characteristica universalis*, a project that occupied Leibniz throughout his life, represents an attempt to create a list of all the basic concepts of thought and to make their combinations notable through symbolic expressions. Leibniz wrote: "I thought that it would be necessary to invent a kind of alphabet of human thoughts and, by linking its letters and analysing the words that are made up of them, to discover and evaluate everything else" (W IV, 47). The idea is that "with the help of numbers, signs and a kind of new language [...] all concepts and things should be brought into proper order". This *characteriscica universalis* should "contain at the same time the art of finding and judging" (W IV, 43).

One would thus possess "a new instrument which will increase the capacity of the mind far more than optical glasses do for the visual acuity of the eyes" (W IV, 53). Thus, in fact, the procedure of a mathematical logic and its symbolic language is anticipated. But the *characteristica universalis* is at the same time more: If one starts out from Leibniz's philosophical premise of understanding reality as a unity of all relationships and interactions of the individual many, a function of the general characteristic as a symbolic language becomes clear which goes beyond the formalizability of thought—because, according to the basic idea, it makes it possible to *uncover* connections and make them comprehensible. This is what is meant by the talk of performance capacity, which is greater than that of the lens in seeing. The *characteristica* does not magnify an object or section of reality, but it multiplies the graspability of relationships in the overall context. At this point, it becomes clear that not necessarily always the logic of signs can lead to metaphysics, but also vice versa a metaphysical problem can lead to the discovery of new forms of thinking.

This does not mean that Russell's argument is completely wrong, but that it is one-sided. For the system of sign language envisaged by Leibniz is supposed to be a powerful method of *ars combinatoria*. Assuming that Leibniz understands the world as a complex and in its complexity increasing and reorganizing relational unit of many, change must result from recombination of the many who are in relationship. The order of concepts must therefore adapt to this constantly reorganizing order of things by new combinations. One aspect of formalization and symbolization through signs is thus to make this new language more powerful due to the size of its task. Leibniz placed great hopes in the *Characteristica universalis*. Whether such a project of putting together basic concepts whose combinatorics would express *all* the changes in reality and make them representable could actually succeed must be marked with question marks. This combinatorics would correspond to a huge "world computer".

Ernst Cassirer and the "Folds of Consciousness"

In Leibniz research, it has been repeatedly stated that the course was set at the beginning of the twentieth century. First because of the discovery of the logician by Russell and Couturat, but also because of the extensive monograph by Ernst Cassirer from 1902. It is often emphasized that Cassirer, too, took logic as his starting point for interpreting Leibniz. This is only correct if one considers the completely different understanding of logic on which the New Kantian Cassirer bases his investigations. In the succession of Kant, logic is transcendental, that is it investigates the conditions of the possibility of cognition. In New Kantianism, this critical question of the conditions of the possibility of knowledge then becomes a philosophical programme of transcendental foundation of the sciences. And it is precisely from this perspective that Cassirer approaches Leibniz.

The title of the book *Leibniz' System in its Scientific Foundations* already articulates the programme: to trace the unity of metaphysics and science at Leibniz. The entire introduction is dedicated to Descartes, for he made "the indissoluble mutual relationship of philosophical and scientific thought" (Cassirer 1902, p. 3) the basis of modern philosophy. This is the fundamentally correct framework in which Cassirer places his interpretation of Leibniz. The problem begins when he interprets Descartes almost in terms of transcendental philosophy for many pages (almost as a precursor of Kant), interpreting his philosophy as an *epistemological* foundation of mathematics and natural sciences and then also understanding Leibniz in this direction. There is no doubt that modern metaphysics is the foundation of science—but one should not hastily judge these different forms of the foundation of scientific thinking and the determination of the relationship between philosophy and science by the classical philosophers of the seventeenth century from the premises of a transcendental logic or, in the case of the Neo-Kantianism, a transcendental theory of science. This narrows the view of the differences.

The presentation of Leibniz' metaphysics then logically begins with the "problem of consciousness" (Cassirer 1902, p. 355). Cassirer's description of Leibniz's concept of consciousness is entirely influenced by Kant: "The *relation* of a manifold content to a unity that expresses and represents it is the constitutive moment in Leibniz' definition of consciousness. In this purely relational character all 'being' that we can add to the term is exhausted." And even more clearly: "According to its most general meaning, the ego is first of all merely the expression of a *relational basis* that precedes all being" (Cassirer 1902, pp. 356 and 358). It is to this perspective on Leibniz's metaphysics that questions must be directed: Does it make sense to understand it from the perspective of consciousness, since Leibniz's concept of consciousness, unlike Kant, does not, to speak with a distinction of Cassirer, represent a *function,* but is what it is in *substantial* relations. This relationship structure is primary, and consciousness does not face it constitutively, but stands within it and expresses it.

Certainly consciousness is central to Leibniz, because only through consciousness can relationships come to themselves. Cassirer refers to this, for example, when he reads Leibniz's concept of apperception in Kantian: Leibniz "prepares the tools for Kant's concept of '*apperception*'". And thus he becomes Kant's forerunner: "In Leibniz' analysis of the concept of consciousness, the material of the problems arose, whose formal mastery and whose uniform principle of solution is only achieved in critical idealism"

(Cassirer 1902, p. 370f.). The spontaneity of consciousness, which in Leibniz's case is to be understood from the interplay of active and passive force, is brought close to a transcendental, that is formal, principle for consciousness activity. It is the same problem that we already saw with Russell: something correct is seen, but from its own systematic preconditions it is one-sidedly pointed in a direction of which it remains at least questionable whether it does justice to its object of investigation.

An intensive examination of the problem of consciousness takes place in Leibniz's *Nouveaux Essais*, a work that Cassirer translated not by chance. In the introduction to this translation, he also reads Leibniz's examination of Locke through Kant's glasses, when he states as the theme of the book the "question of the origin and validity of our knowledge" (Cassirer 1971, p. IX). In his examination of Locke, however, Leibniz is not concerned with the logical identity of "I think", which must be able to accompany all my representations (this is Kant's later definition of transcendental apperception), but with understanding consciousness as something gradual, namely

> that at every moment in us there is an infinite number of perceptions without conscious perception and reflection, i.e. changes in the soul itself of which we do not become aware, because these impressions are too small and too numerous or too uniform, so that they do not show sufficient distinguishing features in detail. Nevertheless, they can have their effect together with others and, as a whole, at least in a confused way, bring themselves to perception. Thus, the habit of not paying attention to the movement of a mill or a waterfall leads us to ignore it when we have lived very close to it for a while. (W III.1, XXI)

Leibniz does not want to deal with Locke's empiricism of perception with the abstract rationalism of Descartes' *cogito* (not even in a logically more refined form, which the argument takes on in Kant's transcendental apperception), but rather points to the embeddedness of conscious being in conditions that surround it in order to get to the actual core of the determination of consciousness. The states, which range from the unconscious to the semi-conscious to a clear content of consciousness, have their basis in the *active directionality* of all consciousness, and it is precisely in this theory of the active intellect, which comes from Aristotle, that Leibniz's main argument consists of against John Locke's idea of the *tabula rasa*, according to which the impressions are imprinted on the mind like on an empty wax slab. In this accentuation of consciousness as an activity lies, of course, the limited right of Cassirer's interpretation; but the one-sided interpretation of this activity as a quasi-anticipated transcendental principle obscures the not inconsiderable differences between Leibniz' and Kant's view of human consciousness.

For Leibniz is not concerned with the logical identity of the ego, but with showing that the ego *individuates* itself through its self-activity. The activity of the consciousness consists in visualizing certain perceptions through attention (which also means to fade out other perceptions partially or completely). Consciousness is thus the ability to actively organize the sensory impressions. The soul is not, as Lockes' metaphor of the wax tablet suggests, the sum of its impressions of reality, but a configuration of these impressions and its directed striving to organize the sensory material. For Leibniz, this unity of receiving and acting elements is called apperception, and it *individuates* consciousness. This is something quite different from Kant, who excluded the empirical ego from consideration in fundamental questions and only allowed the logical identity of the ego to be regarded as then transcendental apperception.

The distinction between passive and active mind goes back to Aristoteles (2016, p. 167ff.). Aristotle speaks of a *suffering* mind, that is a mind that receives impressions, and—we freely express the Greek wording here—an *all-producing* mind. Leibniz asserts this distinction against Locke: "I will be countered by the axiom recognized by philosophers that there *is nothing in the soul that does not come from the senses*. But one must exclude the soul itself and its affections from this. *Nihil est in intellectu, quod non fuerit in sensu,* excipe: *nisi intellectus ipse*" (W III.1, 101f.).

This Latin phrase crystallizes the highly topical basic argument that Leibniz puts forward against Locke's empiricism: There is nothing in the mind that has not previously been in the senses—except the mind (and its 'all-producing' activity) *itself*. In its own activity, the consciousness *structures* itself around reality and thus becomes an *individual* identity with a history: "One can even say that by virtue of these small perceptions, the present is pregnant with the future and loaded with the past, that everything fits together. These imperceptible perceptions also denote and constitute the identical individual" (W III.1, XXV). Consciousness, by organizing these perceptions, summarizes them into the unity of an apperception. This, as I said, has nothing to do with Kant, who knows identity only as the logical identity of "I think", but not as the individual reality of coherent contents of consciousness with a *coherent* history.

Leibniz has a beautiful and famous metaphor for this: the folds of consciousness. *The fold* is not simply, as a postmodern interpretation would suggest, a characteristic of the Baroque era (Deleuze 2000), but has a well-defined meaning in Leibniz's consciousness theoretical argumentation, for it is the counter-metaphor to Locke's wax tablet: Leibniz presupposes that in a dark room

> as a pictorial surface, there would be a canvas, but it would not be completely flat, but divided by folds which would represent the native knowledge: that, moreover, this canvas or membrane, when stretched out, would have a kind of elasticity or effectiveness, and that it would even have a certain activity or reaction, which would be based both on the old folds and on the new ones resulting from the impressions of the pictures. And this activity would consist of certain oscillations and wave movements, such as one would perceive on a stretched string when touching it, in such a way that it would produce a certain musical sound. For we do not only receive the images and traces in the brain, but also form new ones from them when we consider the *complex ideas*. So the canvas that represents our brain must be active and elastic. (W III.1, 181)

This quotation summarises the essence of Leibniz's argumentation: consciousness is elastic activity, and its folds are caused by its own activity. Consciousness thus *forms* the structure through which everything else is perceived, and this means that consciousness *restructures* itself in the course of its activity, and thus has a history which it cannot leave behind because it has entered into structuring, but which can still be further changed by further directed activity. Finally, the image of vibration has the metaphorically exact meaning that consciousness not only suffers something—like the pressure on the string—but at the same time, out of this external pressure, it acts into its environment (in this case, swings or sounds). The elasticity of the string in this interplay is what Leibniz wants to assert against the completely mechanical and one-sidedly conceived relationship between being and consciousness in Locke's work. Current brain research and cognitive science could certainly do more with this view of consciousness as a fold, since it is now scientifically proven that the structure of the brain is formed from its activity and interaction with the environment, because it is in this interaction that the neuronal connections are formed that make each of us what we are.

Regarding Cassirer's appropriation of Leibniz's thoughts for a *transcendental* conception of consciousness, it must be said that it can only account for one aspect: the spontaneity or free activity of consciousness. This spontaneity is recorded by Kant as the essential function of consciousness in general. The very fact that Leibniz understands it not as an abstract principle of "I think", as Kant did, but as an activity *on another*, leads rather to the Hegel of the *Phänomenologie des Geistes* (*Phenomenology of Spirit*)—a book that also deals with the development of consciousness in relation to reality and not with spontaneity merely in opposition to it. Anyway, the metaphor of the folds of consciousness refers to the fact that consciousness is essentially produced by the development on the other. It is an *individually* formed structure of perception and thought. Just as the life of an aging person is expressed in the folds of his or her face, the folds of consciousness are an image for the structure of human experience.

Hans Heinz Holz and the Discovery of the Dialectician Leibniz

Hans Heinz Holz's monograph on Leibniz, which we have already quoted in the revised and greatly expanded version from 2013, was first published in 1958. It is important to note this in order to correctly understand the historical context of this "perspective" on Leibniz. In 1946, the year after the end of the Second World War, Leibniz's 300th birthday was commemorated in many academic events and publications. The coincidence of the anniversary brought to light, to use Walter Benjamin's famous expression, Leibniz's "now-time". His thinking, too, fell into the post-war period after a catastrophic war of the century. In 1946, he was considered the thinker of peace and was generally perceived more politically than before and also afterwards.

The occupation of Holz with Leibniz falls into this time. Contrary to the general tendency of the *Zeitgeist* of being critical with metaphysics, he developed a *metaphysical* and at the same time *political* interpretation of Leibniz's philosophy. This is a further perspective on Leibniz, because it illuminates Leibniz from the systematic starting point of dialectic. The philosophical-historical classification of Leibniz in a history of the problems of dialectic (Holz 2011) goes beyond the scope of this book. We only want to trace the basic idea where Leibniz's metaphysics of the unity of the relationship of the many touches on basic statements of dialectic.

The basic thesis is the unity of substance aspect and structural aspect in the monad model:

> Leibniz grasps the essence of 'structure' (even if this term does not yet appear in his work) much more radically than the modern 'structural theorists', whose concept of structure has grown out of isolated ontic partial contexts. His concept of structure (called 'substantial form', as we will see in a moment) states that all relations into which being enters, allow precisely this being to *be,* and that this form of relations *is* the unity of being. [...] For, all that exists is already inserted into superordinate structures and only exists within these structures. The highest concrete structural concept is then *world*, whereby world is nothing other than the epitome of all real and possible mutual conditions and relationships that connect inner-worldly being with each other and determine it according to its essence. (Holz 2013, p. 41 f.)

The unity of substance and structure as a core thesis means nothing less than making Leibniz a classic of dialectic. For that relations are not accidental and external to the existing but essential to it is an ontological basic thesis of dialectical thinking. In other words: Relationality is intrinsically included in the concept of being. Hence, the talk of structure does not, either, mean structuralism (in the sense that, in this line of thought, the structure of an area of reality—for example, language—is extended to the description of reality in general), but is the title for the unity of relations in which every individual being has always been. Structure thus becomes a general ontological determination for a reality that starts out from the individual, substantially individual and is simultaneously understood via its mutual relations.

This is only apparently a contradiction: traditional terminology understands substance to mean the stable, independent and farsighted, whereas a relationship always expresses dependence. Structure, on the other hand, comes terminologically originally as *structura* from the Roman building industry and means the construction of a building, that is something composed of parts. The substantial (the plurality of the many individual beings) is, however, only one, albeit essential *aspect* of being, which only acquires reality in the contexts of the relationship unit, which as structure constitutes the other aspect.

As Holz puts it: "That which structures itself is also the structured, in any case the world as a whole. For this complicated situation, Leibniz offers the concept of substance, which he based his ontology on, conceptually modified. Substance is that which enters into the structure as a material link, but at the same time also that which, as the totality of the links, is itself a structural unit" (Holz 2013, p. 42). The "totality of substances is in a relationship of all-round dependence on each other", and this structure "guarantees the substantiality of the world as a unit of these relations" (Holz 2013, p. 43). The unity of individual autonomy and interdependence in the context of the whole, as expressed here, is indeed, as we have seen above, a basic idea of Leibniz's metaphysics. By stating totality as a relational unit of everything with everything, this metaphysics meets a basic concern of dialectic.

Now, however, dialectic had so far (in antiquity through the late and new Platonic tradition) and after Leibniz also with Hegel still exclusively been thought as *conceptual dialectic*. Holz now tries to use Leibniz's philosophy for a *theory of dialectic based on an ontology of the real*. With Leibniz one can not only express the whole as a relational unit logically and conceptually, but also speak of *relations of being*: "In that the monad is not only determined as *perceptio*, but also as *appetite* [...], a dialectic is released on the ground of the structure-substance-relationship", which understands the world whole as "interrelation of action and efficacy of the individual substances" (Holz 2013, p. 53f.).

Even in this case, we cannot enter into a discussion about whether such a position is legitimate or not. However, it can be stated that Holz, unlike Russell and Cassirer, does not use a part of Leibniz's philosophy in order to interpret the whole of his conception, but starts out from the basic approach and core of Leibniz's metaphysics as a whole and only then holds it up to the foil of dialectical thought structures. This makes the positions distinguishable, and it takes account of Leibniz's basic ontological concern to understand the world as a relationship unit of a plurality of substantial individuals. Whether this can then legitimately be called "dialectic" is a matter for each reader to decide for himself, because this interpretation is also a hypothesis.

Unity in Diversity: Leibniz Today

When asked about the consequences that Leibniz, beyond his reception from the eighteenth to the twentieth century, still has for our time in the twenty-first century, one could look for quick answers and say, for example: as the inventor of binary arithmetic, the mathematician Leibniz is one of the intellectual fathers of computer science and thus of the computer age in which we live. That is certainly not wrong, but it is still not enough. We have also already seen that scientific discoveries that cannot be clearly assigned to a name as a theory, as in the humanities or social sciences, can lead to the same result in different ways. The priority dispute between Leibniz and Newton on the question of the authorship of the infinitesimal calculus is an outstanding example of this. The development of computer technology would probably have been possible even without Leibniz. In contrast to classics such as Marx or Nietzsche, who had a *direct influence* on social movements and cultural developments through their thoughts beyond philosophy and science, classical thinkers such as Leibniz, who tended to influence developments within the boundaries of their sciences, appear much more indirect and mediated. It is therefore difficult to say what consequences Leibniz had for reality in the twenty-first century.

Another example not yet mentioned: Leibniz can be regarded as the early discoverer of the insurance industry. Although the Hanover Fire Fund was not founded until 1750, it was based on ideas and mathematical model calculations by Leibniz, which he also used, incidentally, when considering a pension fund. He had developed the idea of a fire assurance in a memorandum to Duke Ernst August, but his forward-looking ideas had not been followed, as so often in this matter. As interesting as this anecdote may be, it makes the same point as in the case of computer technology: insurance companies would certainly have been founded even without Leibniz.

However, there is a philosophical aspect to this case that seems worthy of consideration: for Leibniz's political philosophy complements the principles otherwise fundamental in the political theory of his century, such as self-preservation and freedom as the pursuit of self-interest, with the idea of solidarity and the common good, which is the very foundation of a community of insured persons based on solidarity. Not in the sense of a consequence, but very much in the sense of the normative significance of Leibniz's philosophically founded basic political model for our time, one can therefore speak of the *relevance* of Leibniz's thinking for the problems of the twenty-first century: his insistence on *unity in plurality* and his idea of an *order of compossibility in this plurality* can provide criteria for the political thinking of our time. In conclusion, therefore, we are not so much asking about the consequences, but rather about the relevance of Leibniz's understanding of philosophy and the concept of the political that arises from it.

Today, we must start from the plurality of the many and *at the same time* think the whole, because more than ever everything is connected and interdependent. The only philosophical system that allows this unity to think is laid down in Leibniz's metaphysics.

Philosophy as an Own Form of Theory

In a sense, the history of modern philosophy could be written from the perspective of its loss of own competence. At the beginning of the new age, it left physics or the mathematically understood natural science, and metaphysics as a discipline of philosophy was no longer cosmology and philosophy of nature, no longer a *summa* that thought about God and the *ordo* of the world, but it became a discipline of knowledge justification. This was already a step of philosophy's self-limitation to a kind of theory that was oriented towards the model of scientific knowledge. In the course of the rapid success story of the sciences, the history of these losses of competence continued. Seen from the perspective of the history of science, modernity is an acceleration process of increasing specialization of knowledge; philosophically, it is a process of increasing outsourcing of fields of knowledge from the integral perspective of philosophy; this continues until psychology in the early twentieth century.

So the question to philosophy in our time must be What is left of its own competences, which *cannot be* disputed by the sciences? How does it determine its relationship to the sciences? In the twentieth century, its answer was to become the philosophical foundation of scientific knowledge: Epistemology, philosophy of science, logical analysis of language, metatheory of the sciences in general, a critical reflection on the different conditions of the possibility of knowledge in different areas of science. This is an undeniably important function of philosophy in the age of science. However, it has led to the fact that the *form* of philosophical knowledge has increasingly assimilated to the forms of knowledge of science. A legitimate question, however, is whether there are genuinely philosophical questions that *cannot be* answered by scientific procedures.

One such problem is the question of the *overall context*, that is of what must necessarily be lost to the fragmentation of knowledge, but which cannot simply be put aside—for we live in one world, and especially today in the globally networked twenty-first century in *a* world of ever closer relationships and interactions. Among other things, we cannot do without knowledge that *integrates* philosophical competence and provides a *foundation* in the context, because it is a prerequisite for our orientation in reality.

Leibniz is the godfather of precisely this. The obvious topicality of his understanding of philosophy is already present in the Rosental anecdote: Leibniz describes how he endeavours to adapt to the new mechanical leading science, but in doing so comes up against questions that cannot be answered by the methods of science, but which require a recourse to metaphysics and traditional classical philosophy. For Leibniz, science and metaphysics must be seen in their complementarity. He is a scientist, but he sees that scientific *explanation* and philosophical *justification* are different forms of theory. In contrast to the closed system form in later German idealism, Leibniz is so connectable and topical for the present because he comes from science and the speculative system form is not constructed in a closed way, but is understood as an *open hypothesis* starting from scientific problems. Leibniz's example shows that philosophical statements must not contradict the results of the sciences—and his metaphysics also shows that philosophical thinking does not make explanatory propositions, but rather statements that substantiate the many integrating forces of a *basic idea*.

Therefore, one can certainly question the prohibition of metaphysics that was so widespread in the twentieth century and ask: Are we really living in an age of "post-metaphysical thinking", as Habermas expressed it? It is true that Kant, with great influence over the past two centuries, restricted the use of reason to objects that are given to us in experience. But he had also seen that beyond this area of individual experience, reason is "bothered" by questions that it cannot scientifically answer, but which it cannot "reject" either. One of these questions is the *whole* or the *unity* of experience: "Although, however, an absolute whole of experience is impossible, the idea of a whole of knowledge according to principles is in fact that which alone can provide it with a kind of unity, namely that of a system, without which our knowledge is nothing but a piecework" (Kant 1983d, p. 238). Philosophy in the sense of a systematic theory form is then the foundation of this unity.

Kant's awareness of the problem of the irrefutability of metaphysical *questions* is obviously missing Habermas, when he heralds an epoch of "post-metaphysical thinking" and "bends the philosophical thinking" to the "exemplary claim of the sciences" (Habermas 1988, p. 14). Those who have familiarized themselves with Leibniz's thinking will hardly be able to share the labeling of metaphysics as an "emphatic" theory, and also the fundamental political identification of metaphysical thinking with a "wave of restoration" (Habermas 1988, p. 17) is short-sighted and against this background hardly tenable. Habermas states: "Only under the premises of an unagitated post-metaphysical thinking does this emphatic concept of theory disintegrate, which should make not only the human world but also nature from inner structures understandable. Henceforth the procedural rationality of the scientific procedure decided whether a proposition could be true or false at all" (Habermas 1988, p. 14). No one today wants to return to the former metaphysical way of thinking. Habermas, however, lacks any awareness of the fact that there are questions that methodically guided research cannot even ask, let alone answer. If one does not want to leave such questions to religious faith, but insists on their rational treatability, one will not be able to avoid also in the future to fall back on structures of reason of a genuinely *philosophical* theory form.

Nobody wants to deny the achievements of scientific procedural rationality. If, however, it is made the *only* form of theory, this means an exclusion of questions that aim at the context of the whole, the "whole of experience". Leibniz' example clearly shows us that one can be committed to the scientific obligation to methodically secure knowledge without having to renounce metaphysical questions. It was the discoverer of infinitesimal calculus and the inventor of a calculating machine and horizontal wind power who posed the radical philosophical question: "*Why is there anything at all and not nothing?*" (W I, 427). Leibniz shows us that, although we do not know the whole thing, we can and even must think if we want to develop a coherent world view. He also shows us that a basic idea like the monadological world model can have an integrating function even for scientific thinking.

Philosophy has this integrating orientation function by developing models to think the context of the real. This is not in contrast to experiential knowledge, but complements it. Only a concept of world opens up horizons in which the realms of experience are not fragmentarily delimited from one another, but are related to one another and can be entered into an overarching context. By thinking the unity of the many, the philosophical form of theory acquires a heuristic function for science, but also for man's practical handling of his reality. We have seen how Leibniz's awareness of scientific, technical and political issues was determined by his basic philosophical position. The topicality of Leibniz's concept of philosophy consists in being able to think of the *one* world as a unity of the many. Not against, but in contrast to the accumulated scientific knowledge, philosophy must be an "integrating thinking", which allows orientation in the globalisation processes potentiated by the digital revolution and its potentiation. We live in *one* world as never before. And at the same time, we live in a world of which we no longer have an integral concept due to the progressive specialization of knowledge. This makes Leibniz' philosophy a point of departure for thinking in the twenty-first century.

The Relevance of the Concept of Freedom

In the context of modern philosophy, freedom is understood as the ability to move or determine oneself independently and autonomously. One must therefore distinguish between negative freedom (as independence *from* something) and positive freedom (in the sense of the ability to *do* something). Negative freedom is about external conditions that must be given so that self-determined action can be taken, while positive freedom reflects on the inner conditions of the acting person himself. Only those who can choose are free, and that means spoken on both levels of meaning. External conditions must not be allowed to block the choice, and the person must have the ability to make decisions. Metaphysically turned to the fundamental, this question leads to the problem of freedom of will, which ultimately pushes back the question of objective conditions of action in favour of the idea of an absolute freedom that lies in the will itself. In philosophy, this metaphysical idea of free will goes back to Augustine and is first generally held in modern times by Descartes, then in ethics classically by Kant. The moral value of our actions, according to the quintessence of the categorical imperative, consists *solely* in the autonomous self-determination of the will as the unconditional determining factor of the person, which must happen without regard to external conditions.

In Leibniz's century, it was Hobbes who, in a way that was fundamental to political philosophy, tried to formulate a concept of freedom that claimed to do without metaphysical preconditions. Freedom is essentially the negative freedom of an absence of physical coercion (which can actually be meant both physically and politically): "Liberty, or Freedome, signifieth (properly) the absence of Opposition; (by Opposition, I mean externall Impediments of motion) [...] And according to this proper and generally received meaning of the word, A Free-Man, *is he, that in those things, which by his strength and wit he is able to do, is not hindered to doe what he has a will to*. But when the words *Free*, and *Liberty*, are applied to any thing but *Bodies*, they are abused; for what is not subject to Motion, is not subject to Impediment" (Hobbes 2003, p. 166f.). This is early modern mechanical materialism, which has become tradition-building for empiricism and analytical philosophy.

Its *political* consequence is that "in all kinds of actions, by the laws praetermitted, men have the Liberty , of doing what their own reasons shall suggest, for the most profitable to themselves." (Hobbes 2003, p. 169) Freedom is the absence of coercion, and it is essential for the conception of the political that the question of the positive definition of freedom (according to its preconditions and criteria) is faded out. The political is the framework within which each individual can do what he wants in a selfish way. If one adds to this idea the maxim of a minimal state, which is very widespread today, one has the neoliberal idea of private egoism as unhindered as possible.

Leibniz is opposed to both sides of the freedom theory: to the *abstract* metaphysics of absolute freedom of will, because it disregards all conditions, and to the *exclusively* negative concept of freedom as the absence of hindering conditions. Chapter 21 of the *Nouveaux Essais* is entitled "Possibility and Freedom" and represents a highly differentiated reconstruction of the conditions and degrees of freedom. This already begins with the fact that the French text knows three words for different levels of meaning of the connection between possibility and freedom: *possibilité* means *formal* possibility, *puissance* means the *real* possibility passively present in the existing, and *faculté* finally means possibility as *active capability* (W III.1, 241).

Leibniz makes precisely these distinctions for the concept of freedom: there is formal freedom, real degrees of freedom in an objective context of conditions—and finally active freedom as the ability to do something. It is precisely these levels that the chapter on freedom sets apart, and again Leibniz begins his treatise with a reference to Aristotle: "One can say that the *(real) possibility* [*puissance*, J.Z.] is generally the possibility [*possibilité*, J.Z.] of change" (W III.1, 243). And the active possibility he then immediately calls "*capability*" [*faculté*, J.Z.], that is that which, as realization of possibility, brings about change.

Leibniz clearly rejects metaphysics at exactly the point where Kant will later accept it almost exclusively: in the question of freedom of will. For here, we are dealing with bad, namely abstractly posed questions: "One has good reason to be surprised at the strange way in which people torment themselves with the treatment of misunderstood questions. *They seek what they know and do not know what they are seeking*" (W III.1, 267).

Whoever asks for freedom of will, basically already knows that he is free. What he does not know is that this freedom is not grasped and realized in abstract principles, but in the concrete network of relations of the conditions and possibilities in which the human capacity for free action stands. In this context, Leibniz raises a very important question, namely "whether there is a real distinction between the soul and its faculty" (W III.1, 253). It makes no sense to ask for a being of the soul in itself: it is what it can do and what it does. This is, of course, mentally related to the metaphysics of force points. The essence of substance is force—and as a conscious faculty this force is free action of the soul. If its expression of force is restricted, the soul suffers. However, it is nothing in itself, but always its ability, which is subject to very specific conditions.

It is astonishing how metaphysically critical the metaphysician Leibniz can be in the theory of freedom: "It seems to me that in actual speech *necessity* should not be opposed to will but to *contingency* [...] One should not confuse necessity with determination, for there is no less connection or determination among thoughts than among movements (since being determined is something quite different from being forced or pushed by compulsion)". (W III.1, 263). Here, the turn against the metaphysics of will *and* against Hobbes becomes explicit: he reproaches the metaphysician of will for inaccurately dealing with concepts, thus opening up a false alternative between absolute freedom and determinism; and in unmistakable allusion to Hobbes' position, he makes it clear that determination must not be confused with mechanical determination (which Hobbes does, however, when he thinks freedom from the movement of bodies). This reflected self-determination in conditional relationships, however, is the middle position of Leibniz, with which he delimits himself from the one-sidedness in freedom theory mentioned above.

Leibniz has summarized his differentiated conception in a few lines:

> The concept of *freedom* is very ambiguous. There is a legal freedom and a factual freedom. *Legally a* slave is not free and a subject is not completely free, but a poor man is as free as a rich man. The factual freedom is either the possibility to want what you should or the possibility to do what you want. You speak of *freedom of action*, and this has its degrees and differences. *In general,* the one who has the greater means is also freer to do what he wants. (W III.1, 255)

Here, the distinction between *formal* and *real* freedom is recorded: Slave and serf are formally, that is legally unfree in relation to their masters; in contrast to the slave-owner society and feudalism, in bourgeois society the poor and the rich are equally free in form. This conception of law, however, abstracts from the differences in real freedom, which is linked to the existence of possibilities and conditions. There the rich are then freer than the poor.

The theoretical differentiation of the real *scope of freedom* is done quite Aristotelian through the concept of voluntariness. In the third book of *Nicomachean Ethics*, Aristotle uses freedom and voluntariness almost synonymously: involuntary is something that happens violently or without knowledge, whereas voluntary is an action whose origin lies in the acting individual himself. The criterion for freedom in Aristotle is the possibility to decide in situations. Thus Aristotle puts the problem of freedom into the context of possibility: for situations are constellations of conditions in which possibilities are chosen by decisions (Aristoteles 1984, p. 99ff.).

Leibniz takes up this intrinsic connection between possibility and freedom. He discusses it using an example: a person is carried into a room while sleeping, which is then locked behind him. There is a person there whom he has long wanted to meet. He wakes up and will now voluntarily stay in the room, although he does not have the freedom to leave it (W III.1, 257f.). He is unfree from the *objective* conditions, but will remain voluntary from the *subjective* motivation. It is ultimately about this distinction of subjective and objective moments of a situation in which margins of freedom can be identified. Ultimately, Leibniz is interested in showing that freedom and dependence are two sides of the same coin.

One is the degrees of freedom with respect to the objective conditions in the circumstances where there is more or less freedom of choice. The other side of Leibniz's concept of freedom is the human self-relationship, that is it concerns the subjective conditions of the choice of an action. Here again the theory of *petites perceptions* comes into play: for if voluntariness is linked to consciousness, but if this consciousness is and can be a merely gradual and never an absolute consciousness, both of external circumstances and of internal drives (desires, inclinations, motives of all kinds), then no decision is entirely free: "Often an imperceptible perception, which cannot be distinguished nor disentangled, makes us tend to one side rather than the other, without any reason being given for it" (W III.1, 277).

For Leibniz, freedom lies in striving for a higher degree of awareness in action. As long as we remain in the unconscious or semi-conscious of dark perceptions, all talk of freedom remains a "parrot's chatter", for "the most beautiful moral rules with the best rules of prudence only make an impression on a soul that is *receptive* to them" (W III.1, 285). Consequently, we become free to the extent that our *relationship* to external reality and our *self-relationship* become more conscious and reflected. Leibniz is not concerned with "making moral prescriptions and teaching", but with *education* towards a reflected relationship to external and internal reality guided by reason, "by acquiring the habit of acting according to reason" (W III.1, 289).

Freedom is therefore always something mediated and never absolute: "The soul has the power to postpone the satisfaction of individual desires and is therefore free to consider and compare them one after the other. This is the freedom of man" (W III.1, 307). Hegel will later call this ability "second nature": the ability of man to satisfy his needs through culture and thus to shape them freely not only individually but also socially. Leibniz has found a very apt description of this difference between the reflected reality of man and mechanical nature: "The striving is like the tendency of the stone, which always moves towards the centre of the earth on the straightest, but not always on the best paths, since it cannot foresee that it can hit rocks on which it will break, whereas it would have approached its goal with more success if it had the spirit and means to make a detour" (W III.1, 293). Freedom is this capacity of man to take detours.

A differentiated theory of freedom is a prerequisite for politics as an order of compossibility: the interlocking of claims of subjective self-determination and a complex structure of conditions and possibilities in the relational unit of the whole is the object of the political. The topicality of Leibniz's concept of freedom consists in being able to think about a merely formal concept of freedom, which today determines political discourse, the complexity of the material plurality of individual freedom aspirations as a relational structure. In a word: Leibniz can think the many without fading out their context as a whole. His metaphysics allows us to think of these two moments as order. This gives his philosophy great relevance in today's globalized world, in which it is becoming increasingly difficult to find political answers to the challenges of the time.

Metaphysics and Politics: The Order of Compossibility

Leibniz's political thinking was not, as with the classic of seventeenth century political philosophy, Thomas Hobbes, interested in a political, that is state order that limited egoistic self-interest in order to secure and make it possible. He did not proceed from the competition of individuals, where according to the famous formula *homo homini lupus* everyone is a wolf to everyone. He did not presuppose the war of all against all (*bellum omnium contra omnes*), but aimed at an order that was oriented towards the *commune bonum*, the common good or the *common* interests of the people.

The originality of his approach lies in the fact that the alternative to the liberal understanding of society is not the subordination of individual claims to any more closely defined community. Rather, Leibniz basically assumes the de facto plurality of individual aspirations for realization, and for him a political order of compossibility consists precisely in regulating these individual claims not only in a *more formal way*, in order to then release them as self-interest, but in a *more material way*, so that as many of these individual forces as possible can develop at the same time. This is done on the basis of the idea of promoting common interests and limiting such self-interests, which exclude other realizations, in favor of the common good. The plurality of interests must be put into political proportion in such a way that they become possible at the same time, that is, they may not agree, but they can coexist. It is hardly necessary to emphasize the relevance of such an approach in a present time in which a society of self-interest has globally produced great and outrageous differences in the distribution of opportunities for development and an advanced destruction of the common foundations of life.

The metaphysical precondition of this basic political position is expressed in the sentence *Omne possibile exigit existere:* everything possible strives for existence (or rather, for realization or development). Leibniz counts this ontological basic principle among the absolute first truths, similar to the proposition of contradiction or variety, which we have already come to know as the basic preconditions of logic. It is impossible to think without them, and therefore they cannot and need not be proved. It is similar with the aforementioned ontological principle: without this principle, that the possible strives towards reality, one cannot think about the existence or coexistence of realities (and consequently no society, because it always consists of coexisting individuals whose claims must be mediated):

> This sentence: Everything possible strives for existence can be proven a posteriori, if one assumes that something exists. For either everything exists, and then everything possible will strive for existence so much that it also exists, or something does not exist; then a reason must be given why something exists before others. But this reason cannot be given other than by the general reason of essence or possibility, which is that the possible strives for existence according to its nature and in particular in relation to its possibility and according to the degree of its essence. If there were not in the nature of the being itself some tendency to exist, nothing would exist. (W I, 177)

Thus the ontological becomes a political concept of compossibility. For Leibniz, the starting point is fundamentally the reality and legitimacy of individual forces, which in their realization and development work until they are limited by other forces. Political action within this basic concept consists in minimizing incompatibilities and promoting compossibility, that is creating an order in which the most different realities can exist simultaneously.

As we have seen above, the *Discours de Métaphysique* had already pronounced the metaphysical basic idea that became the guiding principle for Leibniz's political thinking, namely that substances hinder or limit each other, interact with each other and restrict each other. If we go on to assume that the individual is essentially action, this means that the individual substance that "exercises its power [...] *acts*, and the one that passes over to a lesser degree makes its weakness known and *suffers*" (W I, 101).

Politics must therefore be directed towards an order that promotes the ability to act and reduces suffering. Precisely because the metaphysical idea of compossibility implies that more and more reality (more realisation of possibilities and more relations or interactions between individuals) is created, Leibniz himself points to the problem with which political action is confronted: Since the emerging order tends to become more and more complex, the political answers become correspondingly more difficult.

But Leibniz also reflects this problem of a necessary increase in the complexity of reality both metaphysically and politically in the concept of progress. In contrast to the concept of progress in bourgeois philosophy of the later eighteenth century, which was developed classically by Kant and later Hegel, Leibniz does not conceive of progress as a linear development in time, that is as a historical movement towards an end purpose, but as an increase in reality of the whole in the simultaneity of the present (Zimmer 1999). If one follows Leibniz's basic idea that action and suffering, that is the increase and decrease of realities, are intertwined, there must be ascent and descent, that is progress and regression, in the overall reality. For Leibniz, the real question is not whether there is progressive development in parts of the whole, but how the progress of the whole (i.e,. the increase of reality and complexity in the whole) can be thought of.

He gives an answer to this in the fragment *De progressu in infinitum*: "I say therefore that the rise is the true thing if now a point can be assumed below which it is not possible to descend any further and if after some time, however long it may be, one reaches a higher point below which there is no further descent" (W I, 369). This idea can be illustrated in the image of a spiral (unlike the line that accentuates the link between the idea of progress and the passage of time): backward steps (the arc described by the movement of the spiral backwards) do not come back to a past point, but are a return to the starting point at a higher level. Instead of a simple linearity of progress (a thought of which we now well know that it has become obsolete), Leibniz thus thinks of the integration of regression into further development. Relative regressions enter into the scope of new possibilities.

How is that possible? Leibniz thinks the irreversibility of increase exclusively in the realm of knowledge, that is where change cannot be ignored. Necessary progress (i.e., increase of power and effect) exists only in knowledge, because in knowledge the world increases in capacity, that is in possibilities of effect, "because souls are influenced by everything past" and in this way in every present "all former activities are included" (W I, 371). It is the reflection of experience that can turn even something that has failed into progress. Only in this sense of reflected reality is every present then a point in time, behind which one cannot fall behind, because it means an increase of possibilities of effect and an increase of the complexity of the real.

So it is again the metaphysical basic idea that structures the concept of progress. In knowledge and reflection, efficacy coincides through the relational unity of the whole and action on this whole. This means in any case an increase of possibilities, a more highly structured compossibility. This is also a politically extremely interesting idea: in contrast to the classical philosophy of history, which always understands progress as overcoming what is thought to be retrograde and, so to speak, "leaves" it behind, Leibniz assumes that the past is *integrated* into the present and thus also into the shaping of future development perspectives. This is highly relevant in a global world. For although, we live in an epoch in which one part of social reality (the so-called Western world) is more developed than others, at the same time *all* development tempos and modes are combined in *one* world. In other words: we live, to use Ernst Bloch's expression, in a world of "non-simultaneity" of historical development, in which different historical times coexist in the simultaneity of the present.

One can also speak here of "time layers" in the present (Koselleck 2003). Leibniz's concept of progress does much better justice to this reality of different stages of development that coexist in the present than the classical one, because it measures the question of progress by the criterion of the possibility of development of all parts of the whole. The order of compossibility as a measure of political thought and action means creating conditions of interaction between individual forces under which a maximum variety of coexisting possibilities can develop. An order of compossibility is about enabling forces hindered in their development to gain more reality than they had before. It is about balance: to limit such action that restricts more development opportunities than it releases. Relationships between individuals should be set up in such a way that more possibilities are compatible and can thus become reality at the same time (see Bou Mas 2007). Politically speaking, this statement refers to the highly topical demand to move closer to a world order in which differences in development can be sustainably equalised.

Leibniz thinks, to give a significant example, the relationship of master and servant from exactly this perspective. The servant is a servant (dependent on the master and therefore dependent) because his abilities are not sufficiently developed to be independent. Entirely in the spirit of the Enlightenment he then ties the possibility of abolishing bondage to the "education of man", that is to the "training of his abilities up to complete independence" (Holz 2015, p. 143). As much as this thought may historically have come from the Enlightenment, the right to education in the sphere of the individual still has its actual effect in the social context today. For the development of abilities means the unfolding of a potential of possibility, which implies social development as a compossible—and that means: an increase in reality that adjusts to differences, that is the increasing realisation of people. Leibniz wants to shape the plurality of individual realities in the unity of their relationships in such a way that more and more of their inherent possibilities can be set free. In a fragment entitled "On Public Bliss" it says: "One must ensure that people are wise, endowed with virtue, endowed with a wealth of faculties, so that they know, want and can do the best" (Leibniz 1966/1967, p. 134).

One can see that normative and action-guiding consequences arise from Leibniz' metaphysical basic ideas: compossibility as a political concept demands that the realization of possibilities should be designed in such a way that it allows for maximum human development—and that actions that exclude many other possibilities from realization should be avoided. Leibniz offers clear definitions for this basic idea: "An action must be *refrained from which, in* all probability, will bring about more bad than good in society". And further: "*Good for society* is that which causes more good to one person than bad to another" (Leibniz 1966/1967, p. 131).

In *De Jure et Justitia* Leibniz says that what is right is "what is best in summa when we consider the general good" (quoted from Holz 2015, p. 149). He calls justice "orderly charity or the virtue that preserves reason in man's inclination towards his fellow man" (Leibniz 1966/1967, p. 130). The concept of justice thus has the following defining characteristics: It is not only about a personal *attitude* like charity or virtue, but also about a social *order*. This order must be structured according to reasonable principles, namely to shape the social relationships of people in such a way that, according to the principle of compossibility, optimal possibilities for development and the greatest possible diversity of realized life can come into being.

Closing Words: "The Place of the Other"

There is an impressive document for the character and the way of thinking that shape Leibniz' attitude: It is entitled "The Other's Place" and makes empathy the desirable basis for individual and social action: "*The other's place* is the true consideration in politics as well as in morality." And this both in order to recognize the duties against one's fellow human beings, and in the sense of a rule of political prudence, "to recognize the views that our neighbor may have against us. You never penetrate them better than when you put yourself in their place. [...] This fiction incites our thoughts and has served me more than once to foresee exactly what happened later" (Leibniz 1966/1967, p. 136).

It is also interesting to note the fine distinction between empathy as a moral principle, as a rule of political wisdom and as *compassion* for the situation of the other:

> Thus it can be said that the place of the other in morality and politics is a suitable place to let us discover reflections to which we would not have come without these means, and that everything we would find unjust if we were in the place of the other should seem suspect of injustice. And even everything that we would not want if we were in the other's place should make us pause to examine it more thoroughly. The meaning of the principle is then: do not do or deny lightly what you would wish to be done or not denied. Think more carefully about it after you have put yourself in the place of the other, which will give you the opportunity to make appropriate considerations in order to better understand the consequences of what you are doing. (Leibniz 1966/1967, p. 137)

This principle of empathy can be seen as a consequence of the metaphysical basic idea of Leibniz's philosophy: His perspectivism suggests putting oneself in the place of the Other, because it sharpens the awareness that our point of view—unlike the Archimedean point of the Cartesian *cogito*—is not an absolute starting point that can unhinge the world, but is situated in it, and is also dependent and conditioned by the reference to others. This is also important for a culture of debate (and Leibniz was constantly in discussion either directly or through correspondence). It demands openness to differentiation through objections, and the prerequisite for a good discussion is the insight that one is not entirely right and that even in the distorted perspective of another one can still have something in it that has a reality and thus a truth content.

But the principle of empathy also emerges from the metaphysical premise that being is essentially being in-relation. The one who thinks reality as a unity of relationships in a plurality of individuals will not only think from himself, and not only decide for himself, but will also include the perspective of the other and his needs in his thinking—as a rule of wisdom, because he knows himself in relation to and dependence on others, but also because the fundamental knowledge that the situation of the other depends not only on his own, but also on my actions, morally demands this attitude. Just as Leibniz's liberal attitude must not be confused with political liberalism, his basic insight into the relativity of human action and omission is not identical with philosophical relativism.

Finally, the dialectic of the intrinsic connection between action and suffering, as expressed in Leibniz's metaphysics, sensitizes him to empathic compassion—for it implies an awareness of the necessity and inevitability of suffering. The other side of my actions is foreign suffering, my freedom is dependence of the other, but also the other way round: the actions of the other limit my actions and thus my freedom. The "place of the other" means a change of perspective that makes this connection become conscious. It also shows, however, that the problem presupposes the moral, that is individual level, but at the same time transcends it: for the context of this web of relationships must be ordered beyond the subjective on an objective level, namely in the sense of an order of compossibility in a way that optimizes development and minimizes suffering. The "place of the other" thus articulates universally valid maxims of political action that apply regardless of political convictions (although they clearly exclude some political options, namely such ruthless self-interest).

We live in a world in which the accumulated power of self-interest hinders the forces of the many from developing. We live in a neo-liberal world in which the principle of the primacy of *common* interests over individual interests, which Leibniz made so strong, has been pushed back. We continue to live in a world of a lack of empathy for the increased suffering, the prevented development, and a lack of insight into the necessity of compensatory development. We live in a world of modernity driven into its consequences, and Leibniz warned against it: against Cartesian rationalism he criticized the dissociation of man from the natural context, and already in the Rosental the young Leibniz saw the limits (and thus the dangers) of making the scientific-technical world view absolute. It is fascinating to see how the whole wealth of facets of his thinking is *structured and organized* from *a basic idea*. Leibniz' example shows how productive and necessary metaphysics can be. The insight, not at all hostile to science and technology, that one must think the *connection* between nature and mankind, leads him back to metaphysics. Reality is a constellation of possibilities that is constantly restructuring itself in new orders. *Ontologically*, this means a tendency to increase reality and its complexity.

Compared to the metaphysician, mathematician, scientist and technician, however, the political thinker Leibniz was mostly in the background. In the middle of the twentieth century, the affinity of two epochal war catastrophes led to the link to the peace thinker Leibniz. In the twenty-first century, it is now necessary to rediscover the *political* consequences of the *ontological* basic idea of compossibility. For Leibniz calls for development to be essentially thought out and shaped in terms of two criteria: to unfold more *individual* potentials of possibility on the basis of *common* interests. This in turn concerns the two major challenges of our century: the *global* social question, without whose solution individual potentials cannot develop, and the *global* social relationship with nature, which in its present form is destroying the common foundations of life through the ecological crisis. Leibniz's metaphysics is shaped through and through by the basic idea of sustainable development and gives still valid basic principles to the need to give our world a more just order.

Bibliography[1]

Leibniz Editions in Chronological Order

Leibniz, Gottfried Wilhelm: Opera omnia, ed. L. Dutens. Genf 1768.
Leibniz, Gottfried Wilhelm: Leibnitz deutsche Schriften. Hg. von G. E. Guhrauer. Berlin 1838–1840.
Leibniz, Die philosophischen Schriften, ed. C. I. Gerhardt, Berlin und Halle 1875–1890.
Leibniz, Gottfried Wilhelm: Opuscules et fragments inédits. Éd. Louis Couturat. Paris 1903.
Leibniz, Gottfried Wilhelm: Hauptschriften zur Grundlegung der Philosophie. Übers. von A. Buchenau und Ernst Cassirer. 2 Bde. Leipzig (später Hamburg) 1906.
Leibniz, Gottfried Wilhelm: Sämtliche Schriften und Briefe. Hg. von der Preußischen (später Deutschen, heute Berlin-Brandenburgischen) Akademie der Wissenschaften. Darmstadt/Leipzig/Berlin 1923ff. (die sog. Akademieausgabe).

---

[1] This list does not represent a selective bibliography on Leibniz, but only gives titles that have been consulted or cited. Unless otherwise stated in individual cases, the bilingual student edition of the works of Leibniz (2013) is cited as "W", with the volume number in Roman numerals and the page number in Arabic numerals. This edition is page-identical with the older editions of the bilingual edition of the Wissenschaftliche Buchgesellschaft, so that these can also be used for reading. All titles of other authors are cited in the running text, stating the name, year of publication and page number.

Leibniz, Gottfried Wilhelm: Textes inédits d'après les manuscrits de la Bibliothèque provinciale de Hanovre. Publiés et annotés par G. Grua. 2 Bde. Paris 1948.
Leibniz, Gottfried Wilhelm: Philosophische Schriften. Hg. von W. von Engelhardt, H. H. Holz, H. Herring und W. Wiater. Darmstadt 1959ff. (diese zweisprachige Studienausgabe ist als "Werke" 2013 wieder aufgelegt worden und wird im laufenden Text als "W" zitiert). This edition is quoted in the text as 'W'.
Leibniz Gottfried Wilhelm: Politische Schriften. Hg. und eingeleitet von Hans Heinz Holz. 2 Bde. Frankfurt a.M. 1966/1967.
Leibniz, Gottfried Wilhelm: Unvorgreifliche Gedanken, betreffend die Ausübung und Verbesserung der Teutschen Sprache. In: Albrecht Schöne (Hg.): Das Zeitalter des Barock. Texte und Zeugnisse. München 1968, 45-51.
Leibniz, Gottfried Wilhelm: Novissima Sinica. Das Neueste von China. München 2011.

Further Literature

Aiton, Eric J.: Leibniz. Cambridge 1985.
Antoine, Annette/Annette von Boetticher: Leibniz für Kinder. Hildesheim/Zürich/New York 2016.
Aristoteles: Die Nikomachische Ethik. München 1984.
Aristoteles: De anima/Über die Seele. Griechisch und Deutsch. Übers. mit Einleitung und Kommentar von Thomas Buchheim. Darmstadt 2016.
Baumgarten, Alexander Gottlieb: Metaphysica. In: Texte zur Grundlegung der Ästhetik. Hamburg 1983.
Baumgarten, Alexander Gottlieb: Theoretische Ästhetik. Hamburg 1988.
Benjamin, Walter: Ursprung des deutschen Trauerspiels. In: Ders.: Gesammelte Schriften. Bd. 1. Frankfurt a.M. 1974, 203–409.
Benjamin, Walter: Das Passagenwerk. In: Ders.: Gesammelte Schriften. Bd. 5. Frankfurt a.M. 1982.
Blumenberg, Hans: "Nachahmung der Natur". Zur Vorgeschichte der Idee des schöpferischen Menschen. In: Ders.: Wirklichkeiten, in denen wir leben. Aufsätze und eine Rede. Stuttgart 1981, 55-103
Blumenberg, Hans: Die Sorge geht über den Fluss. Frankfurt a.M. 1987.
Bou Mas, Francesc Xavier: Systematisches Denken und Politik. Zur Leibniz-Interpretation von Hans Heinz Holz. In: Christoph Hubig/Jörg Zimmer (Hg.): Unterschied und Widerspruch. Perspektiven auf das Werk von Hans Heinz Holz. Köln 2007.
Cassirer, Ernst: Leibniz' System in seinen wissenschaftlichen Grundlagen. Marburg 1902 (Reprint Hildesheim/New York 1980).
Cassirer, Ernst: Einleitung. In: G. W. Leibniz: Neue Abhandlungen über den menschlichen Verstand. Übers., eingeleitet und erläutert von Ernst Cassirer. Hamburg 1971, IX-XXIX.

Bibliography 135

Couturat, Louis: La logique de Leibniz. Paris 1901.
Couturat, Louis: Über Leibniz' Metaphysik. In: Heinekamp/Schupp 1988, 57–80.
Deleuze, Gilles: Die Falte. Leibniz und der Barock. Frankfurt a.m. 2000.
Descartes, René: Von der Methode richtigen Vernunftgebrauchs und der wissenschaftlichen Forschung. In: Ders.: Philosophische Schriften in einem Band. Hamburg 1996.
Feuerbach, Ludwig: Grundsätze der Philosophie der Zukunft. In: Ders.: Gesammelte Werke. Hg. von Werner Schuffenhauer. Bd. 2. Berlin 1982, 264–341.
Feuerbach, Ludwig: Geschichte der neuern Philosophie. Darstellung, Entwicklung und Kritik der Leibnizschen Philosophie. In: Ders.: Gesammelte Werke. Hg. von Werner Schuffenhauer. Bd. 3. Berlin 1984.
Garber, Klaus: Martin Opitz – "der Vater der deutschen Dichtung". Eine kritische Studie zur Wissenschaftsgeschichte der Germanistik. Stuttgart 1976.
Goethe, Johann Wolfgang von: Aus meinem Leben. Dichtung und Wahrheit. In: Hamburger Ausgabe. Hg. von Erich Trunz. Bd. 9. München 1981a.
Goethe, Johann Wolfgang von: Maximen und Reflexionen. In: Hamburger Ausgabe. Bd. 12. Hg. von Erich Trunz. München 1981b.
Goethe, Johann Wolfgang von: Studie nach Spinoza. In: Hamburger Ausgabe. Bd. 13. Hg. von Erich Trunz. München 1981c.
Goethe, Johann Wolfgang von: Einwirkung der neueren Philosophie. In: Hamburger Ausgabe. Bd. 13. Hg. von Erich Trunz. 1981d.
Grass, Günter: Das Treffen in Telgte. Eine Erzählung. In: Ders.: Werkausgabe in 10 Bänden. Bd. 6. Darmstadt/Neuwied 1987.
Gulyga, Arsenij: Immanuel Kant. Frankfurt a.M. 1985.
Gurwitsch, Aron: Leibniz. Philosophie des Panlogismus. Berlin/New York 1974.
Habermas, Jürgen: Nachmetaphysisches Denken. Philosophische Aufsätze. Frankfurt a.M. 1988.
Hegel, Georg Wilhelm Friedrich: Enzyklopädie der philosophischen Wissenschaften. In: Ders.: Werke in zwanzig Bänden. Bd. 8. Hg. von Eva Moldenhauer und Karl Markus Michel. Frankfurt a.M. 1970.
Hegel, Georg Wilhelm Friedrich: Vorlesungen über die Geschichte der Philosophie III. In: Ders.: Werke in zwanzig Bänden. Bd. 20. Hg. von Eva Moldenhauer und Karl Markus Michel. Frankfurt a.M. 1971.
Heinekamp, Albert/Schupp, Franz (Hg.): Leibniz' Logik und Metaphysik. Wege der Forschung. Bd. CCCXXVIII. Darmstadt 1988.
Herder, Johann Gottfried: Vom Erkennen und Empfinden der menschlichen Seele. In: Ders.: Werke in fünf Bänden. Bd. 3. Berlin/Weimar 1969.
Hirsch, Eike Christian: Der berühmte Herr Leibniz. Eine Biographie. München 2000.
Hobbes, Thomas: Leviathan (ed. Rogers/Schuhmann). London/New York 2003.
Holz, Hans Heinz: Gottfried Wilhelm Leibniz. Frankfurt a.M./New York 1992.
Holz, Hans Heinz: Dialektik. Problemgeschichte von der Antike bis zur Gegenwart. Bd. III. Darmstadt 2011, 363–580.
Holz, Hans Heinz: Leibniz. Das Lebenswerk eines Universalgelehrten. Hg. und mit einem Nachwort versehen von Jörg Zimmer. Darmstadt 2013.

Holz, Hans Heinz: Leibniz in der Rezeption der klassischen deutschen Philosophie. Hg. und mit einem Nachwort versehen von Jörg Zimmer. Darmstadt 2015.
Huber, Kurt: Leibniz. München 1951.
Jacobi, Friedrich Heinrich: Über die Lehre des Spinoza in Briefen an den Herrn Moses Mendelssohn. Hamburg 2000.
Kant, Immanuel: Versuch einiger Betrachtungen über den Optimismus. In: Ders.: Werke. Hg. von Wilhelm Weischedel. Bd. 2. Darmstadt 1983a.
Kant, Immanuel: Über das Misslingen aller philosophischen Versuche in der Theodizee. In: Ders.: Werke. Hg. von Wilhelm Weischedel. Bd. 9. Darmstadt 1983b.
Kant, Immanuel: Von dem ersten Grunde des Unterschiedes der Gegenden im Raume. In: Ders.: Werke. Hg. von Wilhelm Weischedel. Bd. 2. Darmstadt 1983c.
Kant, Immanuel: Prolegomena zu einer jeden Künftigen Metaphysik die als Wissenschaft wird auftreten können. In: Ders.: Werke. Hg. von Wilhelm Weischedel. Bd. 5. Darmstadt 1983d.
Kant, Immanuel: Über die von der königlichen Akademie der Wissenschaften zu Berlin für das Jahr 1791 ausgesetzte Preisfrage: Welches sind die Fortschritte, die die Metaphysik seit Leibnizens und Wolffs Zeiten in Deutschland gemacht hat? In: Ders.: Werke. Hg. von Wilhelm Weischedel. Bd. 5. Darmstadt 1983e.
König, Josef: Das System von Leibniz. In: Ders.: Vorträge und Aufsätze. Hg. von Günter Patzig. Freiburg/ München 1978.
Koselleck, Reinhart: Zeitschichten. Studien zur Historik. Frankfurt a.M. 2003.
Lessing, Gotthold Ephraim: Durch Spinoza ist Leibniz nur auf die Spur der vorherbestimmten Harmonie gekommen. In: Ders.: Werke. Bd. 3. München 1995a.
Lessing, Gotthold Ephraim: Leibniz von den ewigen Strafen. In: Ders.: Werke. Bd. 3. München 1995b.
Mahnke, Dietrich: Leibnizens Synthese von Universalmathematik und Individualmetaphysik. Stuttgart-Bad Cannstatt 1964.
Mann, Golo: Das Zeitalter des Dreißigjährigen Krieges. In: Propyläen Weltgeschichte. Eine Universalgeschichte. Hg. von Golo Mann und August Nitschke. Bd. 7. Frankfurt a.M./Berlin 1991, 133–230.
Marx, Karl: Exzerpte aus Leibniz' Werken. In: MEGA IV/1. Berlin 1976.
Ortega y Gasset, José: Der Prinzipienbegriff bei Leibniz und die Entwicklung der Deduktionstheorie. München 1966.
Plessner, Helmuth: Die verspätete Nation. Über die politische Verführbarkeit bürgerlichen Geistes. Frankfurt a.M. 1974.
Poser, Hans: Gottfried Wilhelm Leibniz zur Einführung. Hamburg 2005.
Poser, Hans: Leibniz' Philosophie. Über die Einheit von Metaphysik und Wissenschaft. Hg. von Wenchao Li. Darmstadt 2016.
Russell, Bertrand: A Critical Exposition of the Philosophy of Leibniz. Cambridge 1900.
Russell, Bertrand: Philosophie des Abendlandes. Ihr Zusammenhang mit der politischen und sozialen Entwicklung. Köln 2012.

Bibliography

Schelling, Friedrich Wilhelm Joseph von: Zur Geschichte der neueren Philosophie. Münchener Vorlesungen. In: Ders.: Ausgewählte Schriften. Bd. 4. Frankfurt a.M. 1985, 417–616.

Schopenhauer, Arthur: Über den Willen in der Natur. In: Ders.: Werke in fünf Bänden. Nach den Ausgaben letzter Hand hg. von Ludger Lütkehaus. Bd. 3. Zürich 1988a, 169–321.

Schopenhauer, Arthur: Parerga und Paralipomena: kleine philosophische Schriften. In: Ders.: Werke in fünf Bänden. Nach den Ausgaben letzter Hand hg. von Ludger Lütkehaus. Bd. 4. Zürich 1988b.

Spinoza, Benedictus de: Die Ethik. Lateinisch und Deutsch. Stuttgart 1977.

Spinoza, Baruch de: Theologisch-politischer Traktat. Hamburg 1994.

Voltaire: Candide oder der Optimismus. Mit Zeichnungen von Paul Klee. Frankfurt a.M. 1972.

Wolff, Christian: Rede über die praktische Philosophie der Chinesen. Übers., eingeleitet und hg. von Michael Albrecht. Hamburg 1985.

Wolff, Christian: Erste Philosophie oder Ontologie. Übers. und hg. von Dirk Effertz. Hamburg 2005.

Zimmer, Jörg: Fortschritt als Ordnung der Kompossibilität. Gedanken über Leibniz und geschichtsphilosophische Probleme unserer Zeit. In: Topos. Internationale Beiträge zur dialektischen Theorie 13/14 (1999), 39–59.

Zimmer, Jörg: "Jedes Existierende ist ein Analogon alles Existierenden". Philosophische Grundlagen der symbolischen Weltanschauung Goethes. In: Domenico Losurdo/André Tosel (Hg.): Die Idee der historischen Epoche. Frankfurt a.M. u.a. 2004, 117–127.

Zimmer, Jörg: Vorwort. In: Gottfried Wilhelm Leibniz, Werke, Bd. 1. Darmstadt 2013, VII-XIX.

Zimmer, Jörg: Christian Wolffs Chinarezeption und das Problem philosophischer Interkulturalität. In: Philipp Richter/Jan Müller/Michael Nerurka (Hg.): Möglichkeiten der Reflexion. Festschrift für Christoph Hubig. Baden Baden 2018, 75–87.

GPSR Compliance
The European Union's (EU) General Product Safety Regulation (GPSR) is a set of rules that requires consumer products to be safe and our obligations to ensure this.

If you have any concerns about our products, you can contact us on

ProductSafety@springernature.com

In case Publisher is established outside the EU, the EU authorized representative is:

Springer Nature Customer Service Center GmbH
Europaplatz 3
69115 Heidelberg, Germany

www.ingramcontent.com/pod-product-compliance
Lightning Source LLC
LaVergne TN
LVHW011004250326
834688LV00004B/63